THE JOURNAL OF A GHOSTHUNTER

THE JOURNAL OF A
Ghosthunter

Simon Marsden

TIGER BOOKS INTERNATIONAL

For Tadgh Orlando Marsden

As several of the houses included in this book are private property
and therefore not open to the public, the author asks that
the reader respect their privacy.

The author has made every effort to ascertain the historical accuracy
of the stories retold in this book but, since they are often handed
down from generation to generation, accounts do differ and it has
occasionally been necessary for him to select what seemed
the most appropriate version for reproduction.

This edition published in 1998 by
Tiger Books International PLC, Twickenham, UK

First published in Great Britain in 1994 by
Little Brown and Company (UK) Ltd
Brettenham House, Lancaster Place
London WC2E 7EN

ISBN 1–84056–012–6

Printed in Singapore

Half-title page: Gargoyle, Das Reiche Tor, Bamberg, Germany
Title page: Killua Castle, County Westmeath, Southern Ireland

CONTENTS

INTRODUCTION

The piercing eyes of the grey-haired old man stared ahead at the small gathering of local people. The lights were dimmed and he slowly put his half-empty beer glass down on the wooden table. Not a sound could be heard in the small room except for the occasional crackle of burning wood in the fire and the sporadic coughing of a very frail old woman. He began to speak in a low, measured voice:

'The legend I am about to tell you I heard from my grandfather, and he no doubt from his grandfather before him. It was long, long ago that a great castle in the Burren was lived in by a tyrant chieftain who was crueller than all others. This fearsome lord had but one son, who, unlike his father, was a kind and gentle young man. He lived in terror of his father, but even more so of one room in the castle, which had been cursed, nobody knew when or why. It had always been known as the "Haunted Room" and the door was always kept locked. If any of the family were to sleep in this room, he or she risked hearing the cry of the clan's banshee in the dead of night – an ill omen in Ireland – that would condemn them to sleep for a lifetime or more.

'As time went by, the young man fell in love with the beautiful daughter of a neighbouring chieftain and they were betrothed to be married. But, several nights before the day of the wedding, his friends decided to play a trick on him. Plying him with drink, they slipped a powerful sleeping draught into his goblet so that he fell into a deep sleep. Then, disguised as old men, they forced the lock of the "Haunted Room", carried him in and lay him on the old bed, which was covered in dust and cobwebs . . .

'When he awoke some hours later the young man was full of terror. He believed that he had been asleep for as many years as the curse foretold. His friends, who by now had had their fun, peeled off their masks and began to tease him for believing the curse. But it was too late. The young man's mind had gone. He had lost all reason and was to live out his days in torment, refusing ever to leave the castle. For the rest of his life he was faithfully nursed by his beautiful bride to be, who he always said reminded him so much of his long dead love.'

The old man raised his glass and drained it, then unnervingly stared at each of his audience in turn, adding, 'It is the ghost of the heartbroken young girl that still haunts the ruined tower. It is she, a pale apparition, who may be seen in swirling mist as she wanders sadly through the crumbling walls.'

I had been listening to a *seanchui*, the Gaelic name for a storyteller. It was this chance meeting that inspired me to make my next journey into the unknown.

Tomb in Kreuzkirche graveyard, Zittau, Germany.

Baroque statue in Cluj-Napoca, Transylvania, Romania.

In two of my earlier books on the supernatural, *The Haunted Realm* and *Phantoms of the Isles*, I dealt exclusively with hauntings and other paranormal phenomena that have occurred, or still do occur, in the British Isles. For this book I wanted to concentrate on other European countries, including the little-explored Eastern Bloc. Although less well documented than that of the British Isles, the ghost-lore proved if anything to be more bizarre and terrifying. Little did I guess that my journey would end at Dracula's grave, a place I had no idea existed before I began my travels.

It seemed appropriate to set out from Ireland, which lies at the most western point of Europe, and whose people still respect their ancient past and their strong ties to nature. I intended to finish in Transylvania, which for many people is merely the fictional land of Bram Stoker's *Dracula* but in fact is part of Romania, and which I found to be everything he had inspired in my imagination and more. Everywhere the countryside is alive with suggestions of the supernatural, from the dark Carpathian Mountains with their howling wolves, to the mysterious gypsies and their tales of the *strigoi*, or vampires. Then there is the legacy of the real Dracula, or Vlad the Impaler, whose horrific deeds – far more terrifying than any myth – in the late fifteenth century still haunt his palace and castle. In France, deep in the wild and remote Pyrénées region, the ghosts of the persecuted Cathars, victims of a violent Crusade in the thirteenth century, still haunt their spectacular castles, and a small village in the former state of East Germany is overshadowed by the mummified corpse of the Naked Knight. In the west of Germany I explored Castle Frankenstein, an inspiration for Mary Shelley's Gothic novel, and itself haunted by the legend of a monster.

I remain firmly convinced that a hidden, very different 'spirit world' runs parallel to our own so-called 'reality', and that this other secret existence, which lies concealed behind material appearances, can be revealed to any one of us if the conditions are right and we allow ourselves to be receptive to it by conquering our innermost fears of the unknown. The Celts, for example, believed that human beings could cross over into this 'supernatural world', or 'Edge' as they called it, at certain ancient and sacred sites (see Littledean Hall in England, page 34), and this I believe would help to explain the frequent occurrence of so many paranormal phenomena at these locations.

The author Colin Wilson described the existence of this parallel world with the following analogy: A man is driving at night through the countryside at speed. The car headlights are full on and the radio is playing. Suddenly he slows down to a crawl, switches off the radio, dims the lights and winds down the windows. He is now receptive to a completely different experience of the world, one that is all too often obliterated by the demands and pace of modern-day living. It is in this elevated state, Wilson suggests, that we can be said to be truly alive. I remember reading a book that described how the witches of old would sleep alone and naked in the depths of the dark forest, in the belief that by enduring this trial of fear, they would gain great power over other mere mortals.

We live in an age that is questioning the role and wisdom of modern-day science and its dogma that all life is material. I find it very hard to take seriously the new

A roadside shrine (top) at the entrance to the Red Tower Pass, Wallachia, Romania. Right: Mountshannon, Castleconnell, County Limerick, Southern Ireland.

computer technology of 'virtual reality', which seeks to reinvent buildings of great architectural beauty at the same time as we destroy them; or genetic engineering where man foolishly interferes with nature to create the 'perfect' animal or, worst of all, tampers with human life itself. But perhaps the greatest stupidity and arrogance is being displayed in a multi-million dollar experiment that is scheduled to take place in the USA which, we are told, will reveal the nature of the origin of the universe. In simple terms this will simulate the collision of two planets, the 'Big Bang' as it is known, that is said by many scientists to be how our universe was born. But who, I ask them, invented the planets that collided in the first place?

I was more intrigued by two stories that were told to me by an English painter who now lives in the mountains of the Pyrénées. He has for years collected unusual articles from books and magazines and one of these detailed several recent cases of the imprint of ghostly faces being seen on windowpanes during electrical storms. These images had appeared because certain chemicals, which had collected on the surface of the glass over time, acted like photographic emulsion when originally exposed by lightning, capturing the image of the person who was in the room at that moment. These photographic chemicals can, of course, settle on any inanimate surface and react in the same way when exposed. A second article concerned what is known as 'thermo-luminescence', the method of dating ancient china and pottery. When a piece of pottery, even a household brick, is fired, it takes in the alignment of the magnetic field of wherever it is situated at that time in the world. This information is stored in the crystallization and is revealed by the dating process. What other information could this brick contain, I wondered? Could these concepts also help to explain the 'tape-recording' theory of ghosts, where inanimate objects, such as stone and wood, which are frequently found in ancient buildings, are thought to give off their own individual energy fields, onto which extreme human emotions can be imprinted and then played back when reactivated?

Statues in Neues Palais, Sanssouci, Potsdam, Germany.

We must rediscover the forgotten knowledge of our ancestors and rekindle our sense of wonder in and respect for the power of nature and the mystery of our universe. We should learn to appreciate these simple truths, and also to be aware of our own ignorance: often it is the simplest truths that are the hardest to grasp and only the worldly wise who can fully comprehend them, not the so-called experts in whom we have so blindly put our trust, and who so often know so much about so little.

In the remote, quieter corners of our landscape there is a strange feeling that we are not alone, and as we pass by some ruined mansion or moonlit abbey at nightfall, we know that within the crumbling walls there still lurk dark spirits from the distant past . . . watching . . . waiting.

A graveyard in a Transylvanian village, Romania.

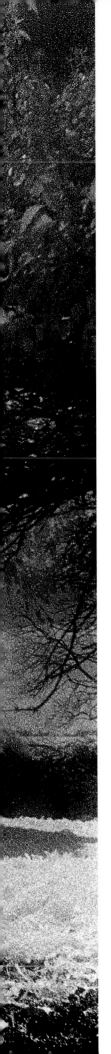

SOUTHERN IRELAND

Now as at all times I can see in the mind's eye,
In their stiff, painted clothes, the pale unsatisfied ones
Appear and disappear in the blue depth of the sky
With all their ancient faces like rain-beaten stones,
And all their helms of silver hovering side by side,
And all their eyes still fixed, hoping to find once more,
Being by Calvary's turbulence unsatisfied,
The uncontrollable mystery on the bestial floor.

'The Magi', W. B. Yeats (1865–1939)

It is said that creative inspiration belongs to a 'universal subconscious' and that certain arcane thoughts exist 'in the air' and can be drawn down by anybody with an open, enquiring mind. Should this be the case then Ireland, with its powerful Celtic legacy, must be a treasure house of the supernatural. Irish writers in particular – Yeats, Jonathan Swift, Charles Maturin, Bram Stoker, Joseph Sheridan LeFanu and M. P. Shiel, to name just a few – have always shown a strong interest in fantasy and the occult. Yeats, for example, was a member of the secret occult society, the 'Hermetic Order of the Golden Dawn', who practised alchemy and magic, and much of his poetry is haunted by supernatural terrors. In some ways, he appeared to prefer the company of the dead to the living, and the Irish in general seem content to live alongside ghosts, fairies and other mythological creatures. In this mercurial land one realizes that the veil between this world and the next is almost transparent. Here myth, legend and reality merge in a 'Celtic twilight' where the ancient spirits summon one from within the ruined castles and the wilderness.

I personally find the country's powerful, mystical aura exhilarating; it has a sense of timeless tranquillity that inspires the soul. It is the people's respect for nature and their reverence of the past that has kept alive so many ancient myths. Every river, lake and mountain has its own prehistoric name, which conjures up legend-filled images of the landscape. This close relationship with the land has also given the population a sense of security that now eludes many of their European neighbours, who would seem all too eager to abandon their inheritance in an often mindless pursuit of modernization.

In the mysterious area known as the Burren, with its many haunted castles and strange landscapes, I found an irresistible magic that both captivated and unnerved me. Elsewhere, the many mansions of the Anglo-Irish seemed to be alive with ghosts and other bizarre tales. The mystical atmosphere of Ireland is said to have affected the English settlers of the seventeenth century, gradually changing their lifestyles as their hearts began to rule their heads. I like to think of Ireland nurturing a subtle insanity, rather than the madness of so-called reality.

SPIRITS OF THE DEAD

The Burren, County Clare

'A savage land, yielding neither water enough to drown a man, nor a tree to hang him, nor soil enough to bury him.'

This description of the area on the west coast of Ireland known as the Burren dates from the seventeenth century and was given by General Ludlow, a commander in Oliver Cromwell's invading English army, as he attempted to subdue the local Irish population. Burren, or *Bhoireann* in Gaelic, means a 'rocky place' and there is no other similar landscape in Europe. Over three hundred million years ago the land lay beneath the sea, and since then, time, and the powers of nature, have shaped the strange, almost lunar landscape seen today. Vast plains of lilac-coloured limestone lie beneath swirls of rock, and caves descending deep into the mountains contain weird stalactites and the bones of bears, reindeer and the extinct Irish elk. Temporary lakes, known as turloughs, appear and disappear as if by magic through holes in the rock. Massive cliffs rise from the sea, and secret valleys connected by ancient green tracks shelter rare plants and wildlife. Man has inhabited this unique area from time immemorial and everywhere his mark can be seen: megalithic tombs and ring forts, castles and ivy-clad towers of ancient clans, deserted villages, high crosses and holy wells.

I spent days driving and walking through the Burren, marvelling at its beauty and silence, but often unnerved by what I found. The elongated limestone rocks appear like hundreds of coffin lids, eerily moving beneath your feet. Deep fissures in the stone lie hidden, covered by earth and grass, and it is all too easy to fall through. What, I wondered, lies hidden below? The many impressive dolmens were once covered by soil too, and here heroes and chieftains were buried in the foetal position, in the 'womb' of mother earth, waiting to be reborn. I often thought that I heard strange noises, as if people were following me, and everywhere I kept finding strange objects, bones, shells, dead animals, sometimes arranged in unfamiliar patterns.

As I explored the landscape I frequently passed the dark and sinister ruin of Leamaneh Castle, which is larger and far more imposing than the many other tower houses that are scattered across this area. It was not until the third night of my visit, when I went to have dinner with two friends from England who have made the Burren their home, that I discovered the castle's history.

A portrait of Máire Rua O'Brien, dated around 1640. Legends of her lust and brutality still haunt the Burren.

Previous pages: Lackeen Castle, Lorrha, County Tipperary, Southern Ireland.

Máire Rua was said to be violent and cruel, and to have hanged any servant who displeased her from the corbels of Leamaneh Castle, a man by his neck, a woman by her hair.

The O'Briens, descendants of Brian Boru the legendary eleventh-century High King of Ireland, were once the dominant clan in the region and Leamaneh Castle was one of twenty-two fortresses that they owned in County Clare during the fifteenth century. The main tower was built in 1480 and a mansion, deer park and magnificent gates were added later. It will forever be associated with Máire Rua, or 'Red Mary' O'Brien, the tempestuous, red-haired she-devil. Born Mary MacMahon, she married Conor O'Brien, the then owner of the castle, in 1639. She would often accompany her husband on his raids against the English invaders, but on 25 July 1651 Conor was ambushed and mortally wounded by Cromwell's men, dying in his wife's arms later that night at Leamaneh. The next morning the courageous lady put on her finest dress of blue velvet and silver braid and drove her carriage into the city of Limerick, where she demanded to see General Ireton, Cromwell's Commander-in-Chief in Ireland. During their confrontation she offered to marry any English army officer who had the courage to ask her. A young standard bearer named John Cooper took up her challenge and she was later reputed to have murdered him by throwing him out of a window at Leamaneh when he was drunk.

The beach below Doonagore Tower is said to be haunted by the ghosts of sixteenth-century Spanish sailors, who survived an Armada shipwreck only to be executed by the local Irish people.

Many such legends surround Máire; how many of them are true we will never know in a country that has such a strong oral tradition. She was alleged to have been a violent and cruel woman who hanged any servant who displeased her from the corbels of the castle, the men by their necks, the women by their hair. She was also rumoured to have possessed an insatiable sexual appetite for both young men and young women, and to have kept a wild stallion in the grounds of the castle, saying she would marry any man who succeeded in riding the animal. Many people believed that she was a witch and there are several versions of how she died. One claims that she was entombed alive inside a hollow tree by her enemies and left to starve to death, another that she was riding from Ennis to Corofin one stormy night when her long hair caught in a branch above the road and she was swung off her horse and hanged by her own hair. Whatever the truth, the spirit of this remarkable woman and the tales of her daring exploits still haunt the castle and the surrounding area.

Amongst the other dinner guests were several local Irishmen, who told me of two other former O'Brien tower houses that are said to be associated with supernatural phenomena: Ballynalackan Castle, where the phantom of an unknown woman has been

This is a haunted landscape where superstition still holds sway and ancient customs live on in the minds of the people.

*The wild scenery of the
Burren is scattered with
ancient monuments:
megalithic tombs,
iron-age ring forts and
ivy-clad towers.*

seen near the archway of the bawn, and Doonagore Tower out on the coast. Here the unfortunate survivors of a Spanish shipwreck at the time of the Armada in 1588 were sentenced to death by the notorious High Sheriff of Clare, Boetius Clancy. Tradition says that he murdered them, and that it is not the tower but the beach below which is haunted by the ghosts of the bedraggled, half-drowned seamen, who had survived one horrific ordeal only to meet a more violent end.

I was then told about the hidden powers within the landscape itself, of people who had mysteriously gone missing for hours, even days, and then been discovered wandering by the side of the road or lost on the limestone plains, disoriented and unable to remember how they had got there or what they had done. Later, my English friend asked me to follow him outside, where he pointed to the starry sky, at the same time handing me a pair of infra-red night-vision goggles like those used by the army on night manoeuvres. I discovered a world I had never seen before: shooting stars, birds of prey and many other creatures of the night. It is a secret world that I had been totally unaware of.

The next day was very hot and I went for a swim before walking through a beautiful valley in the very heart of the Burren, finally emerging near an old farmhouse. A very old man was sitting outside with his dog, seemingly oblivious to my approach. I stopped and asked him about some ancient stones that I had passed about a mile back. He still looked straight ahead and, without changing his expression, said, 'Those are the Druid Stones, where they used to practise the old religion.' Here the history of the people is still alive in the landscape and the unseen spirits of the dead are all around.

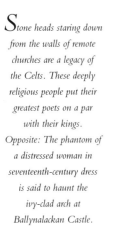

Stone heads staring down from the walls of remote churches are a legacy of the Celts. These deeply religious people put their greatest poets on a par with their kings. Opposite: The phantom of a distressed woman in seventeenth-century dress is said to haunt the ivy-clad arch at Ballynalackan Castle.

A WARNING TO THE CURIOUS

Annagh Castle, Lough Derg, County Tipperary

Appearing like a 'ghost ship' in the night, this ancient castle of the renowned O'Kennedy clan is said to conceal a fabulous hoard of treasure that has never been found. Legend says it was hidden by Edmond Roe O'Kennedy, who rebelled against the English Queen Elizabeth I in the sixteenth century, and was killed at the stronghold along with his secret. Over the following centuries his ghost has appeared to several unsuspecting visitors to the castle. The apparition has been described as deathly pale, with its throat cut, the blood dark and congealed.

A German archaeology student, who visited the site in 1975, told of how, when he was examining the castle vaults early one summer's evening, he heard a gasping sound behind him. Frozen by fear, he waited a few seconds before turning slowly to see a ghastly apparition standing at the top of the steps, blocking his exit. He managed to grab a large rock and hurled it at the spectre, which disappeared into thin air. Some weeks later, on hearing the ghost story from a local man, he could not help wondering whether the spirit was trying to harm him, or perhaps lead him to the treasure.

Tradition says that ancient treasure lies hidden within Annagh Castle's crumbling walls, guarded by the terrifying apparition of its sixteenth-century owner, Edmond Roe O'Kennedy.

A TIME TO DIE

Birr Castle, County Offaly

'Suddenly one day both the clock's weights fell out with a loud bang at what later turned out to be the very hour on which the donor's wife had died. Then, some years later, the whole clock fell forwards onto its face for no apparent reason. This also turned out to be the very hour on which the donor himself departed from this world.'

The face of the grandfather clock was uncannily compelling. I was not surprised to learn that it had been exorcised some years previously as a precaution against the paranormal powers it seemed to radiate.

I was standing in the Great Hall of Birr Castle, listening to Lady Rosse read extracts from the notes that had been written by her mother-in-law Anne Rosse and left inside a magnificent grandfather clock. Now known as the Haunted Clock, it had been presented to Anne Rosse's father, Colonel Leonard Messell, by his Dutch employer in New York on the occasion of his marriage (it even tells the time of the tides in Amsterdam). Messell then brought it back to London, where these extraordinary events had taken place. Years later, the Messell furniture was divided amongst the three children. When they came to decide who was to have the clock, a most sinister crack and groan came from inside the antique timepiece. In spite of this bizarre series of events, it was chosen by Anne Rosse and shipped over to Birr, where it was exorcized by a Father Dean Owen. Since then, there have been no further major disturbances.

The Rosses have always been a colourful family. According to Peter Somerville-Large in his book *Irish Eccentrics*, Richard Parsons, the first Earl of Rosse (who was descended from another branch of the family and who did not, in fact, live at Birr), was a notorious member of the Hell Fire Club in Ireland, and dabbled in sorcery and black magic. The third Earl was an eminent astronomer and in 1847 built a giant telescope in the castle grounds, which can still be seen today. It was the biggest in the world for over three-quarters of a century and through its vast lens he was able to observe and draw objects that were more than ten million light years away. His wife Mary, Countess of Rosse, shared his obsession with the heavens and was an early pioneer in photography. Her greatest ambition was to photograph the moon. It was only in recent years that her darkroom was discovered in one of the castle's towers, the bottles of chemicals covered in dust and cobwebs.

The present Lady Rosse is a painter and an archaeologist and believes that the astronomers of the last century may not have been the first at Birr to take an interest in the stars, the sun and the moon. The castle as it now stands was built over and around the gate tower of a former fortress, the Black Tower, belonging to the powerful and notorious O'Carroll clan. (The O'Carrolls' main seat was at nearby Leap Castle, reputedly the most haunted castle in Ireland.) The hall of the present castle is therefore over the original medieval gateway. On midwinter's day, 21 December, Lady Rosse noticed that the rising sun shines directly through the hall and thus would have shone directly through the O'Carrolls' gateway. One wonders how far back this gateway may date; it is not impossible to envisage that the castle had its foundations on an iron-age ring fort. A direct alignment on the solstice might take this entrance even further back in time to some hidden tomb or ceremonial site.

Over dinner we discussed ghosts and the supernatural. Lady Rosse told me that her husband had always maintained that one of the rooms in the castle was haunted, but would never tell anyone, not even her, which one or why. Later, as we sat beside the great log fire in the library, we agreed how sad it was that we humans seem to question so little of our past, for the past is always present, however much we try to suppress it.

It is conceivable that the original O'Carroll Castle at Birr had its foundations in an iron-age ring fort, or even beyond that to a hidden tomb or ceremonial site.

Lady Rosse's husband maintains that one of the rooms at Birr Castle was haunted, but he would not say which one, or why.

THE PHANTOM PRISONER

Rathpeak House, Ballinasloe, County Roscommon

'When we were children, perhaps eight or nine years old, we all knew that the old house was haunted and would dare each other to bicycle up the driveway, but even in daylight nobody ever went inside the ruin. Our father said a young girl had died a horrible death in one of the upstairs rooms, but never told us why.'

Now seventy-nine years old, Michael Sweeney still lives almost opposite the eerie shell of Rathpeak House. I had been sent to see him by the present owners of the farm on whose land the crumbling mansion stands. They are new to the neighbourhood and know little of its history. Mr Sweeney suggested I contact the county library for more information. In the meantime, I returned to the ruin to take photographs.

I found this place unsettling and longed to know why.

Some months later I received a letter, via the Roscommon Library, from a local historian, Mr Joe Grenham. The following is a synopsis of his letter.

The house was built *c.* 1690 by the St Ledger family, who came from County Cork. Some eighty years later they sold it to the O'Kellys, who were rich landowners in the Ballinasloe area. The male line of the O'Kellys subsequently died out and the house was inherited by the eldest daughter, who married an army officer by the surname of Lynch. This particular branch of the Lynch family came from County Galway and were known as the 'Mad Lynchs' because of their unpredictable and outrageous behaviour. (In the late seventeenth century one of their number became Mayor of Galway City and then proceeded to sentence his own son to death by hanging.)

These new owners of Rathpeak had several children, including a beautiful daughter who fell in love with a lowly ploughman on the neighbouring estate belonging to the Dillon family. The Lynchs were Catholics and the Dillons Protestants, as a result of which there was already a good deal of ill feeling between the two families. The girl's brother, Owen Lynch, a soldier, was a particularly brutal and headstrong young man who, on discovering his sister's illicit affair, shot her lover. The heartbroken girl was then locked in an attic room of Rathpeak and left to starve to death by her tyrannical parents. She endured this torture for several days before killing herself by continually banging her head against the wall. Shortly afterwards, her brother killed a fellow army officer in a duel and was transferred overseas by his regiment. After the parents died, the house changed hands several times before becoming the ruin it is today.

This, then, was the story Mr Sweeney's father had felt unable to tell his children, and is why local people still believe the house to be haunted by the figure of a distraught young girl sometimes seen at an upstairs window. Other witnesses over the years have told of hearing a slow but continuous knocking, followed by an overwhelming silence.

Rathpeak House is forbidding and it was with some relief that I saw it was too dangerous to enter, and that I must content myself with photographing its exterior.

THE HANGING GHOST

Tullynally Castle, County Westmeath

A massive, turreted gatehouse dwarfs the peaceful Irish countryside. Beyond, a long, twisting driveway leads to a vast, castellated mansion surrounded by an eighteenth-century park and pleasure grounds. This is the Irish seat of the Earls of Longford, whose ancestors originated from Suffolk in England and who were granted lands here in the seventeenth century in return for their military services to the Crown. Like so many other Anglo-Irish families, they were soon to fall under the spell of this magical country.

I was greeted by Valerie Packenham, the wife of the present owner, and she gave me a tour of the interior, including the magnificent Great Hall which rises through two storeys of the house. Over lunch she spoke of the family's distinguished history, their military pedigree and how the sister of the second Earl of Longford had married the Duke of Wellington. Now they are cultivating a strong literary dynasty: her husband Thomas is an historian; his elder sister Lady Antonia Fraser a novelist, and their father Lord Longford, the controversial campaigner against pornography, has published several titles.

When I raised the question of whether the house was haunted, Valerie Packenham said that she had heard stories but had never seen anything herself and felt very much at ease with her surroundings. However, there is an elderly lady who has lived for the last twenty years in the east wing of the castle, and she has definitely seen 'something'.

Stone sphinxes stand at the entrance to the gardens of Tullynally Castle, guardians of an ancient twilight world where the ghosts of the past still haunt the ancient demesne.

I spent some time in the company of this charming lady, who told me that many years ago the butler of the household had fallen in love with one of the cooks, but she spurned his advances in favour of another man, and he tragically hanged himself in one of the smaller towers of the castle. The tower has now been converted into a flat. When some tenants saw his ghost in the corridor one night, they left the next morning. She herself had seen the butler's ghost in broad daylight on the roof of the castle, and then again in the gardens, when her dog had gone berserk. The apparition was dressed in a long frock-coat, but she was unable to discern his features.

Some weeks later I spoke again with Valerie Packenham, who said that I should call a friend of hers in Northern Ireland who had recently stayed at Tullynally and seen a ghost. The following is her description of the sighting.

'I had attended a concert with my husband and gone to bed late. At around 2 a.m. I awoke and the room was fairly light as we had left the electric fire on to keep warm. I clearly saw the figure of a young woman, in her thirties, standing by the fireplace staring

at us. She wore Victorian clothes, a black top and a long red dress. As I sat up she faded away to nothing. I was not at all afraid. Since childhood I have seen several ghosts and none of them have frightened me, except one time when I was staying in a house in England and the apparition of a small boy appeared to me. I was later told that he had died in the same room a year before.'

She added that when she had described her experience of the night before to her hosts at breakfast they seemed unimpressed, as if it were merely part of everyday life at Tullynally Castle and entirely unremarkable.

I was told how a butler had hanged himself in one of the smaller towers of the castle. The old lady who lived in the east wing had seen his ghost several times, once on the roof in broad daylight, and more recently in the gardens.

31

ENGLAND, SCOTLAND AND WALES

I seem'd to move among a world of ghosts,
And feel myself the shadow of a dream.
'The Princess', Alfred, Lord Tennyson (1809–92)

As I was born in a country that is thought of as the traditional home of ghosts, and raised in a classically English haunted house that dates from the sixteenth century, I can easily identify with the above lines of poetry. Although I never actually saw our adopted 'family ghost', who was known as the Green Lady, she haunted my childhood and I well remember my father telling us various versions of the story as my brother and sisters and I sat in front of a blazing log fire in the drawing room, our eyes nervously darting glances at the portrait of this phantom Spanish aristocrat that hung over the fireplace.

My father also had an extensive collection of books in the genre and as I grew older I would spend many hours in the library immersed in these tales of terror. My favourites were M. R. James, Arthur Machen, Robert Louis Stevenson and William Hope Hodgson, but then almost all the great British literary figures, from Shakespeare to Charles Dickens, have written about ghosts and the supernatural in one form or another. I also doubt whether it is possible to visit any village or town in the British Isles that does not boast one, or more likely several, haunted houses, and the number of people who claim to have experienced supernatural phenomena is equally impressive. Many of these apparitions appear in ancient houses that have belonged to the same family for centuries, such as Littledean Hall and Kentchurch Court, which are included here. Others surround prehistoric sites such as the Callanish Stones in Scotland, where the Druids practised their mysterious rites, or appear at remote fortresses like Dunnottar Castle as a direct result of its violent past.

Legends of King Arthur and other ancient heroes are still associated with many primeval sites in Britain and elaborately carved figures of mysterious gods such as the Green Man can still be found in churches in the remoter areas of the countryside. But sadly today much of the mystery of our ancient landscape, towns and cities is fast disappearing through property development and intensive farming methods as well as government bureaucracy and the apathy of a general public who, in the main, seem content to accept anything laid before them so long as it is 'new' and diverts them from discovering their present or past. Almost daily we witness historic town houses demolished or turned into banks, churches converted into building societies and supermarkets and golf courses built over ancient burial grounds. All this is justified by the erroneous use of the word 'progress', but it is a fool who denies his or her heritage.

AT THE EDGE OF OUR WORLD

Littledean Hall, The Forest of Dean, Gloucestershire

Littledean Hall must be one of the most haunted houses in the British Isles. It stands on a spectacular upland site overlooking the River Severn, near the edge of the Forest of Dean, where the Order of Ancient Foresters still administer their own arcane laws. The house derives its name from the Dene family, who were Lords of Dene from *c.* 1080 until 1327; the first Lord, William Fitz Norman, held the manor as Guardian of the Forest. The mansion has the remains of a Roman ruin within its foundations and its large cellars date from Saxon times. The present building is Jacobean and in 1984 the current owner, Donald Macer-Wright, whose family has lived here for many years, discovered one of Britain's largest Roman temples in the grounds.

I had made an appointment to meet the owner but, as I had arrived early, decided to view the house from the outside. It is not particularly large but has a distinctly sinister appearance, in contrast to the beautiful gardens. Parts of the house and grounds are open to the public and the old Saxon Hall and stables are now a tearoom for visitors, where I decided to wait for the owner and where I soon found myself discussing the house's ghostly reputation with the lady who serves there. There are times, she said, when supernatural phenomena are experienced almost daily. Only the day before a lady had been terrified by the ghost of a man in cavalier's uniform who walked through a wall where a staircase is known to have been bricked up many years ago, and the week before the wild stamping of horses' hooves was heard in the tearoom. Just then, during her explanation, a door opened and Mr Macer-Wright beckoned me to follow him into the main part of the house.

I felt as if I had crossed a threshold into another world as we spent the next couple of hours combing the dark corridors and dimly lit, panelled Jacobean rooms, rich in atmosphere and riddled with secret passages. Mr Macer-Wright told the various ghost stories with a convincing calm and eloquence that only added to the disquiet that I was feeling. Although few places in the Hall seem to be untouched by ghosts and other unexplained phenomena, two rooms in particular are the centre of these manifestations. The first is the Dining Room, where several tragic events have occurred, not least the death of two brothers of the Pyrke family, who occupied the Hall from the seventeenth century up until 1896. The young men shot each other following an argument over a woman. Two other men, Royalist officers during the Civil War, were killed here in 1644 by Parliamentary soldiers; the spot where they died is still marked by indelible bloodstains. There is also a priest hole behind the panelling near the bay window. This

*P*ortrait of Charles Pyrke (1721–44) with his manservant, known as the Black Boy. It is the Black Boy that haunts the house, causing poltergeist activity.

Previous pages: The Cheesewring, Bodmin Moor, Cornwall, England.

*L*ittledean Hall has few places untouched by unexplained phenomena. One guest room with a four-poster bed, known as the Blue Bedroom, has not been slept in for over forty years because of its ghosts.

leads to a secret tunnel in the cellars below, which in turn was joined to the Grange at nearby Flaxley Abbey. It was through this hidden gallery that a monk would come and give the owners of the hall secret communion when Catholicism was illegal, and his ghost has also been seen in the house.

Hanging above the fireplace is a portrait of Littledean's most famous apparition, the Black Boy. He came from the Pyrkes' sugar plantations in the West Indies and was the manservant of Charles Pyrke, the smart young gentleman who is also portrayed in the picture. They grew up almost as brothers until Charles, at the age of twenty-three, was murdered by the black servant. One story tells how the servant's sister had a baby by Charles, which was why her brother killed his master. Apparently, the baby was also murdered, and the body hidden behind a secret panel in the Rose Bedroom.

The Blue Bedroom, a guest room with a four-poster bed, is reputedly extremely haunted and, as a result, has not been used for over forty years. No one can say exactly who or what haunts the room, simply that if you enter it fills you with an intense feeling of dread.

Mr Macer-Wright then described some of his experiences in the house and one in particular intrigued me. The following is from the written description he later sent me:

'In 1979 I was staying in my boyhood bedroom whilst working on a part of the house to which I was going to bring my family to live. I had no bedside lamp and there were no curtains across the windows, allowing a greyness of light, whatever the time of night. I was woken suddenly by the door slamming, as a man in a violent temper strode across the room to the window, turned and walked back to the centre of the room, where he stopped. His footsteps resonated on the bare floorboards and I could hear his breathing, which was quick and rasping. The room was inky black and I could see no light from the windows. Initially I was extremely frightened, unable to speak out or move. I certainly would not have got out of bed and attempted to turn on the light. When he reached the middle of the room my fear suddenly left me as I realized that the situation was unreal and that this male presence had no idea that I was there. Thinking about it afterwards I found, and still find, it very difficult to resolve whether I was in his time, or he in my time.

'I am totally satisfied that this experience was paranormal and that I was fully conscious; it lasted no more than a few seconds but seemed longer. The moment it was over the darkness evaporated to a normal intensity and I felt totally calm and able to isolate the fact that this apparent male presence walked on the pre-existing floor, not the present carpeted floor, and slammed an earlier door, not the present one with window-panes. Also the room was distinctly wider; there is now an inserted passage. I could, of course, see nothing.'

Mr Macer-Wright left to attend to some business but said he would return shortly. I began to photograph the Dining Room but had to leave as I felt suffocated by the eerie atmosphere. I took the portrait of the Black Boy into the passage to photograph, but was interrupted by the distressed screams of a child coming from the gardens. When I looked out of the window, there was nobody there. Mr Macer-Wright came back and

when he saw my look of unease asked if anything was wrong. I told him what I had heard and he said that visitors often heard such screams. He then went on to say that his family had experienced many different kinds of phenomena over the years and had learnt to accept them. For instance, whenever his youngest son Tom returns home from school, or another lengthy time away from the house, the clocks begin to gain time very rapidly.

We then went outside to the Roman temple, which, he believes, was originally a Celtic shrine to the river goddess Sabrina. The Celts venerated hilltops and springs, and the River Severn, with its great seasonal bores and flood tides, would have been an awesome spectacle to these ancient tribes.

Mr Macer-Wright became more animated now; the subject obviously meant a great deal to him. He has no doubt that this whole area has been a sacred site for centuries, what the Celts would have called an 'Edge'. These were dangerous places where, if you were not careful, you might slip into another 'supernatural world' which we are only aware of in our subconscious. He added that the house itself was believed to be on a ley line and that four or five of these lines crossed in the vicinity, which would produce a strong energy field that could be used for either good or evil. He said that many archaeologists had visited the site over the years, but none of them seemed willing or able to grasp what both he and I believe to be the simple truth: there are more important things here than just man's mark on the landscape; there are also unseen powers that we ignore at our peril.

The owner of Littledean Hall has no doubt that the whole area has been a sacred site for centuries, what the Celts would have called an Edge, where, if you were not careful, you might slip into another, supernatural world, of which we are only aware in our subconscious.

SCREAMS OF THE SHE-WOLF

Castle Rising, Norfolk

The insane screams of Queen Isabella, known as the 'She-Wolf of France', are still said to haunt this massive Norman fortress. One of the most beautiful but depraved women of her time, she was imprisoned here for plotting with her lover the murder of her husband Edward II, whom she had married when she was only twelve years old. She was soon to discover his homosexual tendencies and was jealous of his close relationship with his childhood friend Piers Gaveston. As the barons turned against Gaveston, and eventually Edward, so did she, becoming the lover of the scheming, tyrannical Sir Roger Mortimer. Together they defeated Edward's army and had him imprisoned in Berkeley Castle in Gloucestershire.

A painting of Queen Isabella, the 'She-Wolf', being seized at Nottingham Castle in 1331. She was taken to Castle Rising and imprisoned for twenty-seven years for her part in the murder of her husband, Edward II. Opposite: Queen Isabella's ghostly and insane screams have been heard echoing within the castle's thick walls, some 600 years after her death.

Isabella came to despise Edward and humiliated and tortured him in every way that she could. He was kept in a small, damp and dark chamber containing a well that was twenty-eight feet deep. It was the custom to throw the rotting carcasses of dead animals down the well, which usually meant that the prisoner eventually died of asphixiation or contracted some foul disease that would make it appear that they had died a natural death. But Edward, against all odds, survived this ordeal, only to meet a far more hideous end. Mortimer, with Isabella's consent, ordered his jailors to torture him to death with a hot burning spit. Isabella's son Edward then succeeded to the throne, but it quickly became obvious that he was merely a pawn in Mortimer's hands. Eventually, with great cunning, Edward had Mortimer executed and his mother was seized at Nottingham Castle and taken to Castle Rising.

She was, it seems, quite comfortable in the early days of her incarceration and was frequently visited by both her son and her grandson, the warrior The Black Prince. In time, however, these visits ceased and, increasingly lonely, she began to lose her sanity. She died twenty-seven years after her incarceration, in 1358. Now, even after six hundred years, it is said that her maniacal laughter and remorseful wailing still echo over the surrounding countryside in the dead of night.

I stood and imagined the grim vigil of this cruel woman as she sat alone in one of the castle's towers, but was abruptly woken from my daydream by the sudden screech of circling crows.

VISITORS FROM THE PAST

Kentchurch Court, Herefordshire

H idden away in a secret valley on the border of England and Wales lies Kentchurch Court, the home of the Scudamore family since the eleventh century. I approached the house on a misty winter's morning down the long avenue of elm trees, and felt inspired by an overwhelming feeling of antiquity and the presence of untamed nature.

Once inside the great house Jan Lucas-Scudamore, the wife of the present owner, led me through the Long Gallery that contains an abundance of family portraits, a host of phantoms from an illustrious past. She told me how the family were of French extraction (originally their name was Escudamour) and that they had come to England with William the Conqueror's invading army in 1066, when they were granted lands at Kentchurch. She paused in front of some steps and added that we were now entering the oldest part of the house, the Tower. I felt a definite change of atmosphere inside what is known as Owen Glendower's Room, a dimly lit bedroom with dark wooden panelling and an ornate four-poster bed in one corner. Glendower is a legendary Welsh folk hero who fought against the English in the fifteenth century and one of whose three daughters, Alice, was married to Sir John Scudamore. The family had sympathy with the Welsh cause and Owen was said to have taken refuge at Kentchurch when badly wounded after a bloody battle. A small door in the room opens on to a winding staircase that leads down to some cellars and horses were said to have been kept below so that he could make a speedy escape from his enemies. There is said to be 'something' or 'someone' who haunts this room and the cellars.

*P*ortrait of Jack O'Kent, around 1460. Legend says he was a wizard with supernatural powers.

I then noticed a portrait hanging on the bedroom wall of a sinister, ghostly figure. This, I was told, was the notorious 'Jack O'Kent', whose identity remains a mystery. Some historians say that he was a member of Glendower's entourage, a learned man who had supernatural powers, others that he was a stable lad who had been educated by the Scudamores then sent to France, where he became a Franciscan monk, finally returning to Kentchurch to be the parish priest. Another version says he was Glendower in disguise and that the tales of wizardry were to frighten away any intruders who might reveal Glendower's whereabouts to the English authorities. Whatever the truth, Mrs Lucas-Scudamore said that the painting had become a talisman to the family. She added that when a dowser, or water diviner, had recently visited the grounds he had said that a girl was looking out of this bedroom window and that she was waiting for somebody. This ghost has been seen by several members of the staff over the years.

Later I met the family's nanny, who had lived in the house for over forty years. She had not felt or seen anything unusual, but said that she was not the type of person who would. She did, however, believe that others could and remembered how, when electricity was first being installed in the house many years ago, one man refused to work in the cellars because of something he had seen. She also described how the father of the present owner had stated on a radio programme that only male guests were put to sleep in the 'haunted bedroom' because of something that had happened in the past. She said that the staff were all very surprised by this, as they had not been told before.

A cleaning lady said that she finds the bedroom very unpleasant, always feeling that there is something or somebody behind her. She described how one night, after a shooting party, a very large man was given the room to sleep in. When they took his breakfast to him in the morning he looked very tired and said that he had not slept at all well, because he had heard strange noises. She noticed that he had jammed a large oak chair against the small door to the cellars.

Something or someone haunts the oldest part of the house: the tower.
I felt a change of atmosphere as I climbed the ancient stone steps towards the heavy oak door of the tower's bedroom. Once outside again, the statues gave me the same sense of unease that I had experienced in the tower.

NO ESCAPE

Dunnottar Castle, Kincardineshire

'**O**ver one hundred and sixty men, women and children were kept in the dark dungeon, fed on a diet of rotten meat, raw fish and salt water . . . they huddled together for warmth, their skeletal bodies clothed in rags.'

This was an eye-witness account of the brutal imprisonment of a large number of anti-Royalist Covenanters and their families, who were held at Dunnottar Castle in 1685 by their enemies. Many died of starvation, others when trying to escape at night down the steep cliffs, and some under torture for their fanatical religious and political beliefs. This dark cellar can still be seen today and is known as the Whig's Vault. It is no wonder that this castle in its wild setting on the North Sea, constantly battered by the elements, has a legacy of restless spirits from its violent past.

The castle's isolated position on a huge sandstone rock that towers above the savage coastline would seem to have been impregnable, but it was captured several times and in 1297 William Wallace's Scottish army besieged and destroyed it, burning alive the English garrison in the church. Whether it is their screams and cries that are said to emanate from the rock at night, or those of the pitiful Covenanters, is not known.

The fortress covers four acres and resembled a small village. The many buildings included a barracks, chapel, stables, a priest's house and even an ancient graveyard. The entrance to the castle is through the impressive gatehouse, but there is also a tunnel and steps cut into the rock itself that once gave secret access to the castle. It is near here that the ghostly figure of a man has been seen. He is tall, dressed in archaic military uniform, and he appears to be staring out to sea, as if watching for someone or something.

In 1651, when the Royalist army was close to defeat, Dunnottar was thought to be the strongest and safest location in the land to hide the Scottish crown jewels and other royal treasures from the advancing English army of Oliver Cromwell. In due course the castle was besieged and it became obvious that the hoard must be smuggled out of the fortress before it was captured, to await the King's future restoration. There are several versions of how this dangerous feat was accomplished, but the most widely believed was that the jewels were lowered by rope down the cliff side in the dead of night and hidden under the skirts of a servant girl, who then buried them beneath the floor of a nearby church. There are those who say that some of this treasure is still hidden near the castle.

I stood facing the spectacular ruins from the mainland on a bitter winter's day and noticed the small figure of a lone visitor slowly climbing the winding path towards the gatehouse. As the waves crashed against the seashore and the seagulls circled above like vultures, I thought how vulnerable he appeared in the face of nature's power, and these suggestions of the supernatural.

Dunnottar Castle's isolated position on a huge sandstone rock towering above the savage coastline once made it impregnable. It now lies in ruins, haunted by the restless spirits of its violent past.

VOICES FROM BEYOND THE GRAVE

Kilchurn Castle, Loch Awe, Argyllshire

The romantic ruin of Kilchurn Castle stands at the head of Loch Awe. It was once a fortress of the mighty Clan Campbell, Dukes of Argyll, whose lands these are, and many ancient legends portray its turbulent past. Whilst staying in an old house near the loch, my host recounted a particularly disturbing supernatural phenomenon that had recently terrified a young English couple who decided to camp for the night within the old castle's walls.

'After they had pitched their tent and eaten an evening meal the young man decided to climb the steps of the main tower and watch the sun setting over the still waters of the loch. As he stood facing the window he suddenly felt a "presence" enter the room. Believing this to be his girlfriend, he didn't bother to turn round but started to describe various landmarks to her. Slowly an icy cold began to creep into the tower, as if it were seeping through the thick stone walls and an eerie, pleading voice whispered: "Let me go, please help me to rest in peace, let me go." He was overcome by fear. Then, just as suddenly, the voice fell silent, the temperature rose again and he dared to turn slowly and confront the intruder. But nobody was there. Running back down the steps he found his girlfriend cowering behind a wall. She, too, had heard strange voices that, in her own words, were not of this world. They fled in terror.'

'Let me go,' pleaded the eerie voice, as an icy cold crept into the tower of the castle.

THE SHINING LIGHT

The Callanish Stones, Isle of Lewis, Outer Hebrides

I first saw the ancient stones through an eerie grey mist that was slowly creeping in from the sea. Historians and archaeologists believe that the circle, and its surrounding avenues, were constructed some three to four thousand years ago. The thirteen great stones of the inner circle stand closely grouped, like huge beings in a secret conclave. The tallest, the central pillar stone, guards the entrance to a burial cairn. This was found to contain human bones, which are thought to have been those either of a tribal chieftain or of a sacrificial victim of the Druids.

Some say the stones are men who were turned literally to stone by an enchanter, others that the stones have astronomical connections with the sun and moon, or that they were a ceremonial site. Up until the end of the last century the local islanders believed that on midsummer morning, 'something', described as a 'shining light', would travel slowly down the main avenue of stones to the cairn, heralded by the song of a cuckoo. Perhaps this strange light was the rising sun that had come to reclaim or return the spirits of those who had been ceremonially buried there.

I felt that the stones were drawing their power from some ancient, universal sub-conscious. Why not simply accept that some form of magic is at work, something far more powerful than the mind of man?

Rivalling Stonehenge, the Callanish Stones are a sacred site. For centuries islanders believed that on midsummer mornings a 'shining light' would travel slowly down the main avenue of stones to wake the dead.

THE ESKIMO'S CURSE

Ecclescrieg House, St Cyrus, Aberdeenshire

'Did you ever visit Ecclescrieg?' asked my painter friend over dinner one evening. I was staying with him near Montrose on the Aberdeenshire coast in the midst of a bitterly cold winter. 'Bram Stoker, the author of *Dracula*, used to spend his annual holidays at nearby Cruden Bay and it has been suggested that he used the old house as a role model for Count Dracula's castle.'

'Is it haunted?' I asked him.

The old man thought for a moment, replenished his glass and stared out of the window towards the sea. 'Not exactly,' he replied, 'but there is a strange legend that I have heard people tell about the Forsyth-Grant family who lived there until fairly recently. Their military achievements distinguished them as one of Scotland's most notable families. One of them, Osbert Clare Forsyth-Grant [1880–1911], joined the navy against his father's wishes. He was a wild character with a love of adventure and sailed from Montrose to command a whaling ship off the Arctic coast, manned by a mixed Scottish and Eskimo crew.'

He paused and, turning away from the window towards the roaring fire, continued, 'But at some point, nobody is certain when or why, he earned the displeasure of the Eskimos and it is alleged that they put a curse on him and his family. Shortly afterwards the ship that he commanded, the *Seduisante*, went missing in a storm and was wrecked on a hidden reef. There were rumours of mutiny and killings on board but neither Grant nor any of his Scottish crew survived to tell the tale. The Eskimos had made their way to shore safely, they said, on Grant's insistence.'

I was intrigued by this strange story and very much wanted my friend to continue. 'There is really little more that I can add except that the unfortunate son's place in the family vault still lies empty. His body was never recovered and the great house itself is now deserted and derelict, casting a dark shadow over the village of St Cyrus.' He then remembered that there was still a Commander Michael Forsyth-Grant living in a house near the ruin and suggested that I should try to meet him.

I had little difficulty in finding the commander, who generously entertained me to tea. He showed me many old family papers and photographs and explained how they were able to trace their ancestry as far back as a soldier named Osbert de Forsyth, a standard bearer of King Robert the Bruce at the battle of Bannockburn in 1314. He, however, knew nothing about the Eskimo's Curse. He had been sad to leave the house, but it had become too expensive to maintain. It was now owned by a foreign company, but nobody seemed keen to live there. He gave me a book, published in Canada, about his ancestor's whaling exploits, adding that I was welcome to photograph the house.

Ecclescrieg House is thought to be the model for Count Dracula's castle in Bram Stoker's novel. It now lies empty, some say as the result of a curse put on the family who lived here.

The light was fading fast and the circling crows were cawing as I walked up towards the building. I focused my lens on the broken steps leading to the terrace. I could not help thinking of a passage that I had already read in the book he had given me. It told how, although young Osbert's choice of the sea over the army had so enraged his father at first, many years later, when his ship was reported missing, the old man, who by then was frail and ill, would frequently walk up and down this terrace clutching a pair of binoculars, carefully examining every ship that came into view to see if it was the *Seduisante* – but she never came.

THE KING'S MISTRESS

Roch Castle, Pembrokeshire

Roch Castle has been shrouded in tales of the supernatural since the thirteenth century, when the lands were owned by the Norman family of de Rupe or de la Roche. It is said to have been built on a high rock because Adam de la Roche was warned by a witch that he was destined to die by the poisonous bite of an adder. In its spectacular position above the undergrowth and moorland he felt he was safe from any habitat that might shelter a snake and he became a recluse within the walls of his fortress. But despite these elaborate precautions, the prophecy was fulfilled one stormy winter's night. Earlier in the day his lone servant had carried a bundle of sticks into the castle for the great fire in the hall. That night, after a hearty supper and several goblets of wine, his master fell asleep in front of the flames. An adder emerged slowly from the pile of sticks, crawled across the stone floor and bit the nobleman on the leg. His lifeless body was discovered in the morning.

The castle is also said to be haunted by the tragic ghost of Lucy Walters, mistress of King Charles II and mother of their illegitimate child, the ill-fated Duke of Monmouth, who was beheaded in 1685 for his part in the unsuccessful Protestant rebellion against James II. The Walters were supporters of the Royalist cause in the seventeenth century and the castle changed hands several times during the Civil War. Lucy was a passionate and imaginative young girl who was once described as 'that brown beautiful creature', and she first met the King in Holland, where she had been taken by her then lover, Colonel Robert Sydney.

Lucy Walters, mistress of Charles II, holding a portrait of their ill-fated son, the Duke of Monmouth, who was later beheaded for rebellion.

She and Charles were instantly attracted to each other and enjoyed a tempestuous affair. However, while Charles put his favoured bastard son, the infant Duke, under the care of his wife, he spurned Lucy. She died in poverty at the tender age of twenty-eight. It is said to be her sad ghost, dressed in white, that is seen at the castle, floating through rooms where doors have been locked, and her running footsteps that have awakened the heaviest sleepers in the dead of night.

The castle is now owned by David Berry and his family. They have restored the building over the years, and now it is rented out to visitors. Mr Berry was sceptical as to who or what the ghost might be, but said that several of his tenants claimed to have witnessed inexplicable phenomena here. When I was photographing the castle I was followed by a small, dark-haired girl in a long dress who always stood some distance away in the high grass that swayed in the cool breeze. I spoke to her but she never answered, just kept on staring at me. I finally left the castle grounds through a small gate and followed a tree-lined path to the ancient village church where I had left my car. As I drove away, I caught sight of the little girl again, standing beside a tombstone, still staring after me.

Roch Castle is haunted by the sad phantom of Lucy Walters. She floats through rooms where doors are locked, and her running footsteps wake the heaviest of sleepers in the dead of night.

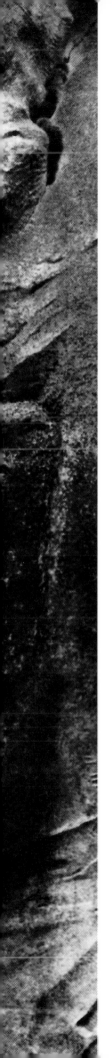

FRANCE

I shall show you what you tried to glean, by the light of tapers,
from the faces of the dead – or when you vagabonded beyond the Pyramids,
in those great sands composed of human remains. From time to time a fragment
of skull turned beneath your sandal. You grasped some dust, you let it sift
through your fingers; and your mind, mixing with it, vanished into the void.

'The Temptation of St Anthony', Gustave Flaubert (1821–80)

Flaubert's haunting prose poem 'The Temptation of St Anthony' explores man's distant past and reveals a grotesque, surreal universe that questions our traditional beliefs and our existence. As I travelled through the beautiful French countryside, I too discovered a fantasy world, of magnificent châteaux that seem to be lost in time, their fairytale towers and classical statues symbols of a lost age of romance and chivalry. Wandering through the richly tapestried halls and ornamental gardens, I imagined the ghosts of their majestic past that are still said to frequent the shadows. The 'Adventure' of the two English school teachers within the grounds of the Palace of Versailles in 1901, when they found themselves transported back in time, seemed plausible but, as in Flaubert's poem, I also found other, darker forces at work around some of these ancient buildings: intrigue and debauchery, murder and suicide, as portrayed in the ghost of the lonely boy at Château de Raray and the infamous Gilles de Rais at Champtocé Castle. These unquiet spirits are still to find the peace of the tomb.

I also photographed many of the Gallo-Roman ruins that still lie scattered across France, the most intriguing being the Pyramide de Couhard, the bizarre funeral monument to a Druid chieftain. But one area of France captivated my spirit more than any other – the wild mountains of the Pyrénées in the Languedoc region. Here, the extraordinary castles of the Cathars and the legacy of their indestructible faith, for which they were barbarously victimized in the thirteenth century, lives on, as do tales of the fantastic treasure that these mystical souls were prepared to suffer and die for. In this remote land the ancient customs and beliefs of the inhabitants still hold sway and death's grim visage, in the form of hideous medieval gargoyles, reminded me of the tortured life and works of the master of the gothic genre, Edgar Allan Poe (1809–49), and the fact that the great French poet Charles Baudelaire (1821–67) devoted almost a lifetime's work to translating Poe's haunting stories and poems into French. But the Frenchman's own poetry can also send a shiver down the spine:

In every climate Death admires you
In your contortions, o'Humanity,
And perfuming herself as you would do,
Into your madness blends her irony!

'Danse Macabre' from *The Flowers of Evil*

AN ADVENTURE IN THE PAST

The Palace of Versailles, Paris

O n 10 August 1901 two conventional English academics, Miss Charlotte Moberly and Miss Eleanor Jourdain, decided to visit the palace and gardens at Versailles, and in doing so unwittingly stepped into one of the most controversial ghost stories ever documented. Having viewed the magnificent rooms in the palace, the two women went out into the grounds and began walking towards the Petit Trianon, a residence that had been built in 1762 for the mistress of Louis XV, and which was later used by Marie Antoinette. After a short while they realized that they had lost their way and also that the gardens seemed curiously devoid of other tourists. Then they came across two men who, dressed in old-fashioned coats and three-cornered hats, appeared to be gardeners. When Miss Jourdain asked them the way they replied in a very curt manner, but the two women followed the path that they had indicated. It was at this point Miss Moberly later stated in her diaries that she became overtaken by an extraordinary depression, a fact that she did not reveal at the time to her companion. At the very same time Miss Jourdain, according to her diary, was assailed by an almost overwhelming sense of loneliness and began to think that she was sleepwalking. She, too, kept silent about these feelings.

*M*iss Moberly (left) and Miss Jourdain in middle age.

They went on to encounter several other figures in period dress around the gardens, including a cloaked man sitting by a kiosk at the edge of some woods. Miss Jourdain described how he turned towards them as they approached, but she felt that he was not really looking at them. She was, however, startled by his evil, pock-marked face. Miss Moberly later wrote how everything around her 'suddenly looked unnatural, therefore unpleasant. There were no effects of light and shade, and no wind stirred the trees. It was all intensely still.' On finally reaching the Petit Trianon Miss Moberly saw a pretty, fair-haired woman, again in old-fashioned clothes, who was sitting on a seat in the garden and appeared to be sketching. A few minutes later they entered the mansion and were soon mixing with other tourists, who were dressed in twentieth-century attire. The vision or spell was broken.

It was not until a week later that the two women felt able to compare their experiences, not all of which were similar. Miss Jourdain had not seen the lady sketching, but they both agreed that something very strange indeed had happened to them. During the following ten years they individually made several return visits to Versailles, but found the landscape and atmosphere very different from their original trip. Buildings had disappeared; some paths that they had walked down were now blocked by brick walls, and

Previous pages: Carving on tomb, cemetery of Père Lachaise, Paris

*E*ach statue seemed somehow to be alive as if a guardian of the palace's past. Some, like this small boy riding on a serpent's back, had a hypnotic effect, disturbing the already surreal atmosphere.

As I walked down the long, tree-lined avenue towards this magnificent fountain at the Palace of Versailles, I felt as if I were in another world, one of beauty and tranquillity, where time stood still.

where the lady had been sketching there was now a large rhododendron bush. They made extensive researches into the original design of the gardens and the style of dress of the people they had encountered. The evidence seemed uncanny but they both came to the same conclusion: somehow they had been transported back in time and what they had witnessed was life at the palace *c.* 1780, just before the French Revolution. It was then that they decided to publish an account of their extraordinary experiences, and wrote *An Adventure* (1911).

The book caused great controversy and many experts in the paranormal, including the Society for Psychical Research, were critical of much of its content. However, other witnesses who claimed to have had similar experiences at Versailles began to come forward, and the arguments raged. Then, in 1965, Phillipe Jullian published a biography of the French dandy Robert de Montesquiou which seemed to explain away the whole story. He suggested that the ladies had merely witnessed a fancy dress party, organized by a Mme de Greffuhle, which had been held near the Petit Trianon. However, it has since been established that this party took place in 1894, seven years earlier than the visit of the two English women, and a letter from Madame de Greffuhle proves that she was, in fact, in London on the day of their 'Adventure'. The affair remains as great a mystery today as it was then.

I do not believe that time can only be measured on the scale of seconds, minutes, hours and years. This is Linear Time, a human invention and a mere convenience for the society we have created. It is more likely that the human brain, memory, imagina-

It occurred to me that the haunting landscape of Versailles must have been witness through the ages to many acts of intrigue, treachery, love and death, and it seemed plausible that the critical events are somehow imprinted on the surroundings.

tion, whatever name one likes to give this faculty, is capable of 'seeing' into the past or future when the constraints of linear time are lifted. When I wandered through the gardens at Versailles I became absorbed in their history, from the time of Louis XIII, who chose the setting for his hunting lodge 'to avoid sleeping out in the cold any longer', to Louis XVI and Marie Antoinette, who stood together on the balcony to face the advancing army of peasants who were demanding their arrest and execution. This haunting landscape must have been witness through the ages to many acts of intrigue, treachery, love and death. It seems very plausible that most or all of these critical and emotional events are somehow recorded or imprinted on their surroundings, in the manner of a tape or photographic film, for the sensitive and enlightened to witness at a later date.

Miss Moberly later wrote how everything around her 'suddenly looked unnatural . . . There were no effects of light or shade, and no wind stirred the trees. It was all intensely still.' Both women came to the same conclusion: somehow they had been transported back in time and witnessed life at the Palace of Versailles in 1780, just before the Revolution.

ANCIENT POWERS

La Pyramide de Couhard, Autun, Burgundy

The beautiful French city of Autun was once known as the 'sister and rival of Rome'. It lies surrounded by many reminders of its glorious past and it was whilst climbing the steps of the amphitheatre on an uncomfortably hot summer's afternoon that I first caught sight of a mysterious pyramid on the summit of an adjacent hill. At first glance it seemed no more than a pile of stones, but its shape and prominent position suggested something more, and I hurried back to my car. Following several narrow and twisting country roads, I soon found myself in the small and ancient village of Couhard, where I left my car near the church.

I began to walk towards the curious monument. There was not a person in sight. The grass was overgrown and the area near the stones sadly degraded by the debris of modern-day man. The pyramid itself is about forty feet high, made of irregular stones cemented together. In the middle is a recess that now lies empty. I spent about an hour taking photographs and all the time I felt as if someone or something was watching me. All I saw, however, were several dead birds and the outline of a dog or large cat lurking in the near bushes. I was convinced that this must be some kind of important death monument, but built by whom, and for whom? Perhaps the church would provide a clue.

Just as I was about to enter, a middle-aged man approached me and I asked him what he knew of the origins of the pyramid. He told the following story.

The pyramid stands on the summit of a very ancient cemetery known as the Field of the Urns and there is universal agreement that it is an important tomb or funeral monument that dates from Roman times or even before then, but archaeologists and scientists can agree on little else, despite the numerous excavations that have been carried out over the years. There are also numerous theories as to who is buried or commemorated there; the cavity was believed to have contained a large, ornate urn filled with their ashes. Ancient chroniclers favour two possibilities: Cavare, an eminent King of the Gauls, or Diviciacus, another Gaulish chieftain who was a Druid and a friend of both Julius Caesar and the Roman philosopher Cicero. My companion believed the latter.

'This Diviciacus claimed to have the powerful knowledge of nature,' he said, 'and was recognized as a magician and soothsayer by his people. This Celtic doctrine also professed a belief in the immortality of the soul, which could transmigrate into all living things, including animals and birds.' The man then lowered his voice and spoke of a strange 'force' or 'energy' that was believed to surround the pyramid and of occasions when unsuspecting visitors or passers-by had been rooted to the spot by it. Other stories tell of a strange shape, neither human nor animal, that has been seen in the vicinity of the stones and is said to guard the monument.

Tradition has it that the pyramid was once sixty feet high, covered with shining white marble encrusted with black stars. A twisting stairway led to the summit and on certain ceremonial occasions a bronze urn containing the chieftain's ashes was displayed there.

ALONE

Château de Raray, Picardy

One night, about twelve years ago, I was at a dinner party in Paris where I had a long conversation with a film director who was particularly interested in the fantastic and the supernatural. We discussed a script that I was writing and he was trying to think of suitable locations in France where I might be able to shoot it. 'Have you ever been to Château de Raray?' he asked. I said that I had not and he continued: 'It was chosen by Jean Cocteau as the location for his masterpiece *Beauty and the Beast*, and is truly a fairytale mansion, surrounded by enchanting statues and set in magnificent grounds. It is only some forty miles north of Paris.' He later added that he believed that it was haunted and that the story, if he remembered it correctly, concerned a young girl, a servant of the château in the seventeenth century, who had hanged herself in the woods near the house. She had had an affair with either one of the members of the family who lived there, or another member of the staff, who had rejected her. The tragic part of the story, however, was that her little boy was found wandering in the woods alone, badly injured. It seemed that she had tried to kill him first, but had either not succeeded, or suddenly been unable to go through with the deed. Whatever the truth, the girl must have been deranged at the time and it is this lonely boy's ghost that has been seen in these woods, no doubt still searching for his mother.

I never forgot the conversation, and when the opportunity arose, went to see the château for myself. The night before my visit I reread Charles Perrault's classic fairytale and on my arrival the following morning saw immediately why Cocteau had identified this house with the story. Although the beautiful grounds to the rear of the château are now a golf course and the mansion itself an exclusive hotel, it has been renovated so subtly that none of its majesty has been destroyed. As I walked down the long avenue in front of the château I was exhilarated by the sight of the two extraordinary arcades of statues and busts. On top of the walls are hunting scenes that include no fewer than forty-four dogs, a stag and a wild boar. Beneath them are recesses containing the figures of many Roman emperors and empresses, and Greek gods and goddesses.

In the club house and offices to the side of the château I found a female member of staff who told me some of the building's history, which can be traced back to the thirteenth century and a family called Bouteiller. But the house as it stands today, the grounds and statues, were the creation of one Nicholas De Lancy at the start of the seventeenth century. De Lancy was a councillor to the then King Louis XIII and chamberlain to the Duke of Orléans. She knew nothing about the ghost of the little boy, but did

I spent the afternoon photographing the château and statues. In the bright sun, the shadows on the faces of the ancient gods made them appear like phantoms from the underworld.

The figures on the arch evoke the legendary chase of the unicorn and the arch itself marks the end of one world and the beginning of another.

Château de Raray was chosen by celebrated French filmmaker Jean Cocteau as the location for Beauty and the Beast.

not come from this region of France and said that she was too terrified by the thought of ghosts even to consider that they might exist. However, she thought that I should see the old gateway to what was once the park, known as 'The Gate of the Unicorn', or 'The Red Gate'. She found it very beautiful but unnerving.

I spent most of the afternoon photographing the château and statues. In the bright sun, the shadows on the faces of the ancient gods made them appear like a gallery of phantoms from the underworld. Later, I walked towards the woods and the famous arch. The figures on the gates evoke the legendary chase of the unicorn and conjure up an air of mysticism. Just as I finished taking some pictures, a middle-aged man carrying his golf clubs walked through the arch. Smiling, he asked what I was doing. He said that he found the château, the grounds and the statues a wonderful fantasy world, a great relief from his mundane and oppressive office in Paris. Here, he said, he could relax and let his imagination run wild. I asked him about the ghost story I had been told, but he, too, knew nothing about it. However, towards the end of our conversation, he suddenly looked at me with a more thoughtful expression and said that he remembered an incident that had taken place the previous summer which might be relevant to the ghost of the little boy.

'I had been playing here one weekend with a business friend and my wife had brought our children up from Paris for lunch. The kids then played in the grounds while she sunbathed. Eventually we all met up near the arch and started to walk back to where our car was parked. I asked my four-year-old daughter if she had enjoyed herself, but she shook her head and said no. When I asked why not she took her time to reply, but eventually said that she was afraid of the statues. I told her that they weren't real, so there was no need to be frightened of them, but she said that one of them had moved. "Impossible," my wife said. "But it did, it did," she shouted. "It was a little boy standing in the woods near the arch. He wasn't real." We just ignored her then, even though she was crying. Children are always inventing imaginary beings, aren't they?'

The eyes of each statue sought me out (opposite). If only they could speak, I might learn the truth about the ghost of the little boy. Right: The long avenue in front of the château has two extraordinary and exhilarating arcades of statues and busts, with hunting scenes on top of the walls, and gods and goddesses in the recesses.

GHOSTS OF THE CATHARS

Pays de Cathars, The Languedoc

At the beginning of the thirteenth century the land known as the Languedoc was not officially a part of France and its culture was very different from that of any of its European neighbours. Langue d'Oc means 'The Language of Yes' and this small but unique civilization had created a society that rejected the all too prevalent ethics of the age – the pursuit of personal ambitions through suppression of and violence against fellow men – for the more civilized morals of personal dignity through the love, trust and tolerance of all things. The inhabitants succeeded in creating beauty in all forms of architecture, literature and the arts, and nowhere was this better portrayed than in the cult of the Troubadours, travelling poets and musicians who, through their love songs, preached a message of understanding not force, persuasion rather than conquest.

As this new age of tolerance began gradually to spread through the rest of southern France, Spain and northern Italy, people became impatient with organised religion, especially the Catholic Church, which seemed to be in disarray. All too often it indulged in unseemly acts of pomp and splendour and many of its priests were seen to be leading hypocritical and profligate lives. Out of this disillusionment grew a powerful sect known as the Albigensians, after the city of Albi in Languedoc which was one of their centres, or Cathars, which comes from the Greek word meaning the 'pure ones'. The roots of this faith lay in Manichaean dualism of the third century, which had occult and magical overtones and taught that God and the Devil were equally powerful, and that the material world was a kingdom of darkness created and ruled by the Devil. Into this evil world had come the pure word of Christ who was God's ghostly presence, a holy spirit to be worshipped. According to the Cathars, redemption came not from Christ's death on the cross, but from the example of the life he led on earth. Not believing in intricate and costly ceremonies, the Cathars wore simple robes and were said to have been extraordinarily gentle in their behaviour, their faces reflecting the purity of their souls. The poor people, especially, were able to identify with such a simple faith.

As the Cathars' influence grew, the Church naturally became alarmed, especially when almost the entire aristocracy of southern France became followers of what the Catholic bishops were beginning to describe as a heresy. In 1209, the ironically named Pope Innocent III, with the support of the King of France, called for a crusade against the Cathars. A vast army of knights and mercenaries, many of them English, descended

Les Hérétiques de Montségur by Émile Bayard, 1840. The basis of the Cathar faith was that God and the Devil were equally powerful, and that the material world was a kingdom of darkness ruled by the Devil.

Montségur Castle was the spiritual heart and final refuge of the Cathar faith. On the morning of 16 March 1244, the occupants of the beseiged fortress slowly walked down and submitted themselves to a vast funeral pyre.

from the north of the country to take part in an horrific slaughter and inquisition that was to last for almost half a century.

The Pope had decreed that all those taking part in the crusade were to be absolved in advance of any sins they might commit and that anything of value belonging to the Cathars or their allies would be considered as booty. The Albigensian Crusade began with the siege of Béziers, where the crusaders demanded that the city fathers hand over the small number of Cathars known to be in hiding there. They were refused and the order was given to massacre every man, woman and child of the 20,000 inhabitants. When the Pope's representative was asked how they would be able to distinguish the heretics from the faithful, he answered: 'Kill them all. God will recognize his own.'

The next thirty-five years witnessed some of the most violent massacres since the fall of the Roman Empire. Thousands of Cathars were tortured, left to die in chains or burnt alive for their beliefs. By 1243 almost all recognised resistance had ceased, except for a small number of isolated strongholds, one of which was Montségur Castle. On 16 March 1244, after a ten-month siege, some 200 Cathars were burnt alive here and the fortress and the faith of these martyrs became a legend.

*M*acabre sculptures vividly reflect the violent history of Mirepoix. The town had given shelter to many Cathar heretics. Opposite: Peyrepertuse is a fortress within a fortress, up in the clouds. Its crumbling walls are haunted by a ghostly procession of Cathar 'perfecti', who starved themselves to death rather than submit to the torturers of the Inquisition.

Today, the mystery and spirit of the sect is still alive and the ruins of their castles have become sites of pilgrimage for many people from all over the world. Two of the most impressive and inaccessible of the Cathar castles are Peyrepertuse and Quéribus, high in the Pyrénées. Given their remote positions, it is hard to understand how they were ever captured. Peyrepertuse is a fortress within a fortress, high up in the clouds. Its many crumbling walls are said to be haunted by a ghostly procession of Cathar 'perfecti', the name given to the most holy members of the sect, who are said to have starved themselves to death rather than submit to the torturers of the Inquisition. I doubted whether many visitors would dare to remain within the castle's walls after dark to witness these robed phantoms.

Quéribus is the most dramatic and remote of all the castles. Carved, literally, out of the rock, it appears like some giant's finger pointing towards the heavens. I climbed up the many steps to the fortress on a very hot afternoon, relieved to reach the cool inside of the well-preserved keep with its impressive Gothic interior. Here in the semi-darkness I tried to imagine how these holy men and their loyal soldiers must have felt, cut off from the rest of the world and awaiting almost certain death at the hands of the besiegers. The haunted expression on the faces of two German tourists, who shared the room with me, suggested that they must have been thinking along similar lines. A cold shiver ran down my spine. I began the long climb back down, but this time I felt that

something or somebody was following me. Perhaps it was just a feeling . . . That night I woke screaming from an horrific nightmare. I was imprisoned in a dark cell that was floating somewhere in space. It was filled with skeletons and dimly lit by one white candle that had only an inch of wax left to burn.

Montségur Castle was the spiritual heart and final refuge of the Cathar faith. It had been built on what has always been known as a holy mountain some 4,000 feet above sea level, and in May 1243 it was recorded that there were some 200 Cathars and 300 soldiers within the walls, surrounded by a besieging army of 10,000 men. The siege was to last ten months before, on 1 March 1244, Pierre-Roger de Mirepoix left the castle under a flag of truce to negotiate terms of surrender. It was agreed that all the fighting men would go free, but that the Cathars had two weeks to denounce their heresy, or be burnt alive. During the following days some of the soldiers embraced the Cathar faith,

then, on the morning of 16 March, all the occupants of the fortress slowly walked down from the castle and 216 Cathars willingly submitted themselves to the vast funeral pyre. The site below the castle is known today as the Field of the Burned, and marked by a cross. It is said that this spot is surrounded by a particular force or energy and that a strange white mist has been seen to rise from the ground and drift upwards towards the castle.

Sculptures mock the searchers for the legendary Cathar treasure, which has never been found.
Opposite: I climbed the many steps to Quéribus Castle on a hot afternoon and was relieved to reach its cold interior. But I did not imagine the nightmare this visit would provoke.

One of the many mysteries that surround the Cathars is the whereabouts and the nature of the treasure that they are known to have smuggled out of the castle before it fell. It is said to have been beyond material wealth, but has never been found. It was originally hidden in a fortified cave in the surrounding mountains, but only human bones and skulls were discovered here. Others say that it was taken to sympathizers in a mountain village, where it is still concealed. The extraordinary events surrounding the nearby village of Rennes-le-Château and its eccentric priest (see pp. 73–77) are thought to bear out this theory, but nothing has yet been proved. There are also many theories as to the exact nature of this treasure. One describes it as a book or document that reveals the secret surrounding Christ's death and reincarnation; another that it was the legendary Holy Grail. Richard Wagner is said to have visited the castle when he was writing his opera *Parsifal*, based on the Grail legend, and in the 1930s the Nazis, who perversely believed that they were the rightful inheritors of the Grail, sent a young researcher, a medievalist named Otto Rahn, to Montségur to search for it. He made two lengthy trips, but after the second committed suicide, taking to the grave any secrets that he might have discovered.

The demon Asmodeus, guardian of King Solomon's treasure, holds up the font in the church of St Mary Magdalen. Over the church entrance an inscription reads: Terribilis est locus iste (Dreadful is this place).

THE MYSTERY OF
RENNES-LE-CHATEAU

Rennes-le-Château, The Languedoc

T he tiny hilltop village of Rennes-le-Château has been occupied since prehistoric times and was regarded by the Celtic tribes as a sacred site. During the fifth century it was a prosperous town called Rhedae, an important citadel of the Visigoths, who had toppled the Roman Empire and established a kingdom in the Pyrénées. The stronghold was later besieged and captured from the supporters of the Cathars during the Albigensian Crusade in the thirteenth century. Then, in 1362, the population was wiped out by the plague and the town itself destroyed by Catalan bandits. It never recovered, and remained the small but mystical village it is today.

In 1885 a new curé, or priest, Bérenger Saunière, was appointed. Thirty-three years old, handsome and well educated, but of modest means, he was something of a rebel and was thought to have been sent to this remote village by his superiors as a kind of punishment. For six years he led a very quiet, pastoral life until, in 1891, he started to carry out some restoration work to the village church of St Mary Magdalen. When the top of the high altar was lifted, one of the two sculpted Visigoth columns was found to be hollow. Hidden inside were several wooden tubes containing rolls of parchment. Two of these were

*M*arie Denarnaud *(1868–1953) was confidante and housekeeper to Abbé Bérenger Saunière (1857–1917), the unwitting discoverer of an ancient and controversial secret in the village church that was to change both their lives.*

genealogies dating from the thirteenth and seventeenth centuries, the others were coded documents composed in the eighteenth century by one of his predecessors, the Abbé Antoine Bigou. Abbé Bigou had also been personal chaplain to the Blanchefort family, who had lived at the Château des Seigneurs de Rennes, and who were said to be the guardians of 'a very great secret' passed down from one generation to the next.

Realizing that he had discovered something of importance, but unable to decode it, Saunière took the manuscripts to his superior, the Bishop of Carcassonne, who immediately sent him to Paris to consult with religious experts there. He stayed in Paris for three weeks, mysteriously returning a very rich man, and over the following years continued to carry out secret excavations beneath the church and in the graveyard. He built the villagers a mountain road and installed a water tower at the same time as leading a lavish lifestyle in the company of his housekeeper and confidante Marie Denarnaud, a peasant girl who had worked for him since his arrival in the village. He also built a Renaissance-style house, the Villa Bethania, and a Neogothic tower known as the Tour Magdala. His most remarkable contribution, however, was the elaborate decoration of the church. It was filled with brightly coloured, almost surreal tableaux depicting the Stations of the Cross, strange statues and a bas-relief below the altar that was almost the

Saunière built a Neogothic tower known as Tour Magdala where he kept a large collection of esoteric books and manuscripts. He died on 17 January 1917, and is said to have deeply shocked the priest with his deathbed confession.

exact replica of a stained glass window in a nearby church. All of the figures and paintings, however, contained some bizarre deviation from the traditional version. Another hidden code yet to be deciphered? Above the entrance to the church was a Latin inscription which read: *Terribilis est locus iste (Dreadful is this place)* and immediately inside the door was an horrific statue of a demon holding up the font, which has been identified as Asmodeus, the guardian of King Solomon's legendary treasure.

What had Saunière found and how had he suddenly become so rich? There are only two clues. On his return from Paris after his initial discovery of the parchments, he brought with him the reproductions of three paintings. One of these, Poussin's *Les Bergers d'Arcadie*, together with a tomb in a nearby village, is thought to hold the key to deciphering the codes in the parchments. Another possibility was that he had discovered the secret that had been passed down to the Abbé Antoine Bigou by Lady d'Hautpoul de Blanchefort, the last in line of her family who had lived and died at the Château des Seigneurs de Rennes in the eighteenth century. But what exactly was this treasure or secret? Could it have been the legendary Cathar hoard that was smuggled out of Montségur Castle before it fell to the Crusaders? Was it the vanished treasure of the Knights Templar? (Bertrand de Blanchefort had been a Grand Master of the Templars.) Or was it the gold the Visigoths were reputed to have hidden here? There is, of course, another possibility: it was not treasure, but an ancient secret so important that an organization or individual was prepared to pay a great deal of money for Saunière not to divulge it. Could this have been why he returned from Paris a rich man?

Because of his controversial lifestyle and behaviour, Saunière was eventually suspended from his duties by the Bishop of Carcassonne, but he appealed to the Vatican and was immediately reinstated. Then, on 17 January 1917, at the age of sixty-five, he suffered a stroke and died five days later. He is said to have made a confession on his death bed that so shocked the priest who heard it that he refused to administer Saunière the last rites.

Some time prior to his death, Saunière had transferred his secret and wealth to Marie Denarnaud and she continued to live a comfortable existence at the Villa Bethania. In 1946 she made the Corbu family legitimate heirs to her estate, promising to confide a secret to them before her death which would make them both rich and powerful. But, like Saunière, she died of a sudden stroke seven years later taking, it is believed, the secret with her to the grave.

I found my visit to Rennes-le-Château a very unsettling experience and as I write about it now it seems unreal. Perhaps the sheer weight of mysterious information and imagery is too overwhelming, or the place itself exudes such a powerful energy that one feels both magnetized and repelled at the same time.

In the small museum bookshop I spoke at length with one of the curators who answered many of my questions, although in this village it seems that each answer merely begs another question. She told me how the Tour Magdala was used as a library by Saunière, who had a large collection of esoteric books. She added that the tower, the gardens, and the Villa Bethania are now owned by a Monsieur Buthion. Saunière had

The Church of St Mary Magdalen is filled with brightly coloured tableaux. This bas-relief, below the altar, is the exact replica of a stained-glass window in a nearby church. All the figures and paintings in the church, however, contain a bizarre deviation from the original, or traditional, version.

lived in the presbytery, now the museum, with his housekeeper and only used the villa for entertaining. It is now shut up and she told me that one of the rooms is believed to be haunted and that some previous guests had to leave suddenly in the middle of the night because of something they had seen. An ancient skeleton was discovered in front of the main door to the villa when workmen were digging up the road in the early part of this century.

I noticed a deep hole in the stone floor near where she was standing that was covered by an iron grille. When I asked what this was for, she said it was where a previous owner had dynamited the floor when searching for the treasure. She then added that several ancient legends are linked to the Château des Seigneurs de Rennes, which contains many secret dungeons and passageways. One tells that in the caves that are linked by these underground tunnels live a race of troglodytes, unaware of the passing of time and the light of day.

By now I was mentally exhausted and eager to escape from this waking nightmare. The secret had become too awful to imagine.

THE EVIL LEGACY OF GILLES DE RAIS

Château Champtocé, Maine-et-Loire

Legend tells how, in the winter of 1404, a sudden and violent storm lit up the night sky over Champtocé Castle at the very hour that the wife of Guy de Laval gave birth to a son. Later, as she lay exhausted in the Black Tower, she could never have imagined that this little boy, whom she so lovingly held in her arms, would grow up to be one of the most infamous mass murderers in history.

Gilles de Rais was raised in a privileged world, and both his parents were to die by the time he was eleven years old, making him the heir to a vast fortune. By the age of sixteen he had greatly increased his wealth by first abducting, and then secretly marrying, his cousin, the heiress Catherine of Thouars. This was the first of many scandals that the young libertine was to perpetrate in his short life. Described as a 'youth of rare elegance and startling beauty', he owned many castles and châteaux scattered across France and was soon to indulge in wild extravagances that horrified his fellow aristocrats and dissipated his fortune.

This period of decadence was interrupted by a call to arms from the King of France, Charles VII, who appointed him Marshall of France and Protector of Joan of Arc in 1429. He fought heroically alongside the Maid of Orléans and rarely left her side throughout the campaign. It seems that this extraordinary woman, who claimed to have been called by God to lead the French army, inspired the mystical side of his nature, and when she was captured and burnt at the stake by the English in 1431, he is said to have plunged into a state of self-destructive madness.

Gilles de Rais (1404–40). This sadistic libertine was the inspiration for Charles Perrault's creation, Bluebeard.

Gilles de Rais then retreated to his castle at Tiffauges where he turned to the practice of alchemy, the art of turning base metal into gold, in an attempt to re-establish his fortune. He imported sorcerers from all over Europe to help him with his new endeavours. Under the influence of the most sadistic of these, Francesco Prelati, he was persuaded that to succeed at alchemy, he must enlist the help of the Devil. To do this he must commit the most abominable crimes. It was then that he discovered the grotesque passion that was to consume him for the rest of his life: the torture, sexual abuse and murder of young children, most of whom were boys. It is said that over 200 were sacrificed in his attempt to commune with Satan. In 1440 he was arrested and taken to the city of Nantes, where he was found guilty and sentenced to death by hanging.

I walked up a narrow lane past a butcher's shop towards the castle gates. The old wooden bridge across the moat looked very unsafe. Local people still associate the castle with witchcraft and told me that the spirit of Gilles de Rais could only be exorcized from the building when the last stone had been dismantled and ground to dust.

*C*hâteau Champtocé is dark and forbidding, as befits a place within whose walls such a depraved creature as Gilles de Rais was born. As the shadows began to lengthen I felt myself vulnerable in the presence of such evil.

GERMANY

Now comes upon me long forgotten yearning
For the sweet solemn tryst those spirits keep.
I feel the trembling words of song returning,
Like airs that softly on the heart-strings creep.
The stern heart softens, all its pride unlearning,
A shudder passes through me, and I weep.
All that I have stands off from me afar,
And all I lost is real, my guiding star.

Faust (Part I, Dedication), Johann Wolfgang von Goethe (1749–1832)

Goethe's poetic *tour de force, Faust,* the story of a man who sells his soul to the Devil in exchange for absolute knowledge, was the climax of a lifelong interest in the occult, including the experience of seeing himself as an apparition, or *Doppelgänger.* It happened when he was just twenty-two, as he was parting from his lover.

'As I rode away along the footpath at Drusenheim a strange phantasy took hold of me. I saw in my mind's eye my own figure riding towards me attired in a suit which I had never worn – pike grey with gold lace. Some eight years later I found myself on the very same road, wearing these exact clothes, about to pay one more visit to Frederike.'

I have always considered that there are two parts to the German character: a composed and inscrutable exterior, underneath which lies a powerful imagination. When released, this pours forth genius; take, for example, the paintings of Caspar David Friedrich, the music of Wagner, and the life of the 'Dream King', Ludwig II of Bavaria.

My visit to the ruins of Castle Frankenstein fulfilled a long-standing ambition to confirm the fortress as being one of the inspirations for Mary Shelley's novel of the same name. But it was my travels in the now accessible eastern half of the country that fired my imagination and provided the most terrifying stories. Here, amongst the poverty and pollution of the former communist state, I discovered castles and mansions that had been hidden from the rest of the world for more than half a century. Many of these ancient buildings, such as the castles at Falkenstein and Rothenberg, are atmospherically perched on hills or rocks; others, like Bad Muskau, now lie ruined in their sleepy villages. Only their phantoms of a majestic past linger on. Then, in the remote village of Kampehl, I found the eerie cadaver of a medieval knight that had still not decomposed after 300 years.

But I will be forever haunted by the ravaged city of Dresden, the seemingly endless, bomb-damaged streets, the dark, staring windows and macabrely burnt statues. It was a vision of hell on earth, as if some giant monster had passed through the city, pausing only to suck the life blood from every living creature in its path, before continuing its ghastly journey. What evil, I wondered, could have inspired such a fate?

THE LOST SOUL

Schloss, Bad Muskau, Saxony

On the border of Eastern Germany and Poland lies one of the most fantastic ruins that I have ever set eyes on. Exquisitely carved figures still stand proudly erect on the summit of this vast, romantic monument, having miraculously survived the ravages of the Second World War. The Schloss was once the home of the duke Hermann von Pückler-Muskau, one of Germany's greatest landscape designers and travellers. As a young man, this unconventional aristocrat shocked his contemporaries by entering his family's burial vault at midnight to force open his ancestors' coffins. By carrying out such a dark and macabre deed he hoped to overcome his own fears of death and the unknown. In his old age, he became increasingly eccentric, some say finally insane, and took to driving around his magnificent park in a resplendent, ornate carriage pulled by twelve white deer. On several occasions this entourage was sighted in the streets of Berlin, some 120 miles from his home.

However, according to one of the curators in the nearby museum, it is not his crazed ghost that haunts the ruin, but the pathetic apparition of a beautiful young Abyssinian girl, whose grave can be found in the overgrown village churchyard. It was here, amongst the weeds and wild flowers, that I found her small tomb, which bore a photograph of the unfortunate girl. The protective glass was shattered, the picture torn and covered with dead flies. Below the image was an inscription which read:

'At midday on 27 October the Abyssinian virgin Machbuba died at Bad Muskau Castle. The duke Hermann von Pückler-Muskau had brought her back with him from one of his journeys to the Orient, where she had been living in the high mountains of Abyssinia at the source of the Nile. She was the daughter of a servant of the Abyssinian Royal Family and became a slave of a neighbouring country, who were at war with her rulers. . . . Then Machbuba was sent to Khartoum in the Sudan, where the duke bought her. She was eleven years old. He felt sorry for her and took her back to Bad Muskau as an orphan, where she died of a broken heart at sixteen years of age. Her funeral took place on the evening of 29 October in the village cemetery. All the duke's servants took part in the ceremony, lining the pathway from the schloss to the graveyard, each man and woman holding a flaming torch for the child they had come to love.' *The Church Register*, 1840, no. 51.

Her ghost is still said to wander this lonely route up to the Schloss and sit beneath its crumbling walls. The curator added that the duke always claimed that he bought her to be his daughter, but when he was drunk he was rumoured to boast to his friends how beautiful her young body was.

Duke Hermann von Pückler-Muskau (1785–1871). As a young man he shocked his contemporaries by entering his family's burial vault at midnight to force open his ancestors' coffins.

Previous pages: Monument to Emperor Friedrich Barbarossa, the Kyffhäuser Mountains, Thuringia, Germany.

Among the weeds and wild flowers of the overgrown village churchyard I found Machbuba's small tomb, which bore a photograph of the unfortunate girl. The protective glass was shattered, the picture torn and covered with dead flies.

The Schloss at Bad Muskau is one of the most atmospheric ruins I have ever photographed, the creation of a true genius, now haunted by memories of its resplendent past and the sad phantom of the Abyssinian slave girl who died of a broken heart.

FRANKENSTEIN'S MONSTER

Castle Frankenstein, The Odenwald Forest, Hessen

'I busied myself to think of a story – a story to rival those which had excited us to this task. One which would speak to the mysterious fears of our nature, and awaken thrilling horror – one to make the reader dread to look round, to curdle the blood, and quicken the beatings of the heart.'

This is from the introduction to *Frankenstein,* Mary Shelley's first and greatest work, begun when she was only eighteen years old. Born Mary Wollstonecraft Godwin in 1797, she was the daughter of the feminist writer Mary Wollstonecraft and the political philosopher and novelist William Godwin. Headstrong and highly imaginative, she ran off to France with the romantic and controversial poet Percy Bysshe Shelley in 1814,

Mary Shelley (1797–1851) from the portrait by S.J. Stump.

marrying him two years later when his first wife committed suicide by drowning. Mary was greatly influenced by Shelley's fascination with the Gothic genre and it was in the summer of 1816, when she and her husband were neighbours of Lord Byron and his companion Dr John Polidori in Switzerland, that the seeds of this extraordinary novel were sown.

According to Mary Shelley's own diary it was a very wet and stormy summer and the dissolute quartet of literary geniuses was often confined to Byron's villa in the small village of Cologny outside Geneva. Here, under the influence of alcohol and opium, they would pass the time reading aloud volumes of German ghost stories and it was Lord Byron who issued the famous challenge, daring each of the assembled to write a truly terrifying saga that would frighten generations to come. Several nights later, Byron and Shelley indulged in a long discussion of evolution theories and various other philosophical and scientific doctrines concerning the nature of the principle of life, and the possibility that a corpse might be reanimated, or even more incredibly, that a creature might be manufactured from parts of human bodies and then be given life by scientific means. On going to bed, Mary had a nightmare.

'I saw – with eyes shut, but acute mental vision – the pale student of unhallowed arts kneeling beside the thing he had put together. I saw the hideous phantasm of a man stretched out, and then, on the working of some powerful engine, show signs of life, and stir with uneasy, half vital motion. Frightful must it be; for supremely frightful would be the effect of any human endeavour to mock the stupendous mechanism of the Creator of the World.'

The following morning she began to write her novel, and it was eventually published, after several drafts, in 1818. Today it stands as one of the greatest Gothic horror stories ever written. One mystery, however, remains. How or why did Mary Shelley

According to Mary Shelley's diary the literary quartet would pass the time in Byron's villa in Switzerland reading aloud volumes of German ghost stories. It was Byron himself who issued the famous challenge, daring each of the assembled to dream up a truly terrifying saga that would frighten generations to come.

choose the name Frankenstein for her young nobleman, a medical student, who was driven to robbing graves so that he could put together the parts of dead bodies to create a sad and pathetic monster that in turn hounds him to his own death? It is certainly not a common name in Germany. Did the clue lie in the collection of German ghost stories that was read at Byron's villa? Was there an actual Frankenstein family?

Several years ago a friend lent me a book by Peter Ratazzi called *In Strangest Europe*. In it, I found a chapter, 'In Search of Frankenstein', which mentioned that an ancient family of that name did indeed exist; there was also a photograph of their ancestral home, Castle Frankenstein, which lies in the Odenwald Forest south of Darmstadt.

It is known that Mary Shelley travelled in this region when she was a young girl and I resolved to visit the castle and discover more of the family's history.

Effigy of Anna von Frankenstein, who died in 1566.
Opposite: A legend of the Frankenstein dynasty speaks of a vampire that frequented Castle Frankenstein in medieval times. It is known that Mary Shelley travelled in this region as a young girl, and no doubt borrowed the name for the monster she created.

The ruined walls of Castle Frankenstein are over 700 years old, although two of the towers were restored in more recent times. The fortress was built in 1252 by Konrad Reiz von Breuberg, whose descendants called themselves von Frankenstein. There are several supernatural legends connected to the castle and the Frankenstein dynasty, two of which, ironically, concern monsters. One speaks of a vampire that frequented the castle in medieval times, wandering abroad at night to drink the blood of the villagers, and a young Frankenstein bride who was said to have been found, pale and lifeless, in one of the castle's many towers. The other tells of Georg von Frankenstein, the Dragon Killer, who liberated the people of the valley from the terror of a giant reptile in the sixteenth century. He was mortally wounded in the skirmish and his sepulchral effigy can still be seen in the little church at the nearby village of Nieder-Beerbach, the poisonous lizard beneath his feet. Another striking monument is that of Anna von Frankenstein, who died in 1566. Was it possible, I wondered, that Mary Shelley knew of these legends and that she somehow connected her terrible nightmare in Switzerland with this castle that she had visited, and thus chose the name Frankenstein?

There are other stories concerning the castle. Peter Ratazzi mentions the tale of three young boys from Nieder-Beerbach who, not long ago, unwittingly discovered a series of labyrinthian vaults beneath Castle Frankenstein that seemed to confirm rumours, dating back to the eighteenth century, of the family's hidden treasure. Nothing, however, has ever been found. Another reason why Mary Shelley might have visited the castle was its connection with the famous German alchemist, Johann Konrad Dippel, who was born here in 1673. Could this strange man, whose experiments included the boiling of bones and hair with iron flecks and blood clots, in his search for the secret of life, have been her model for Victor Frankenstein?

Whatever the truth surrounding Mary Shelley's choice of the name, the novel remains a prophetic vision of science running amok in defiance of nature, a theme all too relevant today.

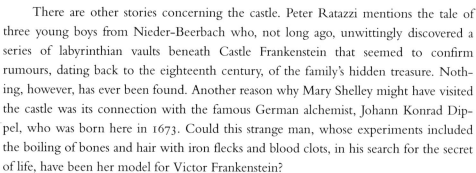

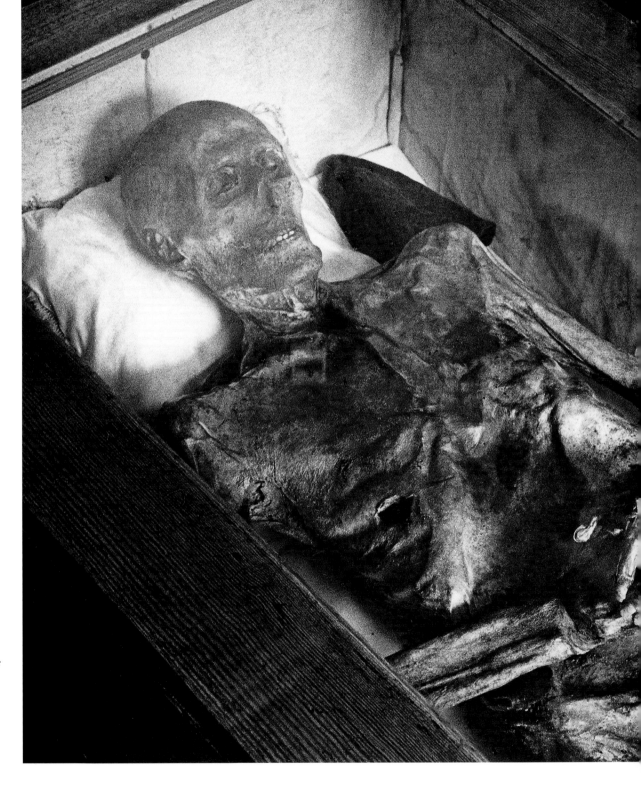

*V*eins are still visible beneath the dark brown hue of the ancient cadaver's leathery skin. I was unprepared for such a sight and clutched the sides of the coffin for support.

THE NAKED KNIGHT

Kampehl, Brandenburg

'His body has never decomposed. I saw it when I was a teenager and can never forget the shock, especially as it was the first time that I had ever seen a dead person. If you are truly searching for the undead then you should visit the small rural village of Kampehl, some seventy kilometres northwest of Berlin, and see this eerie cadaver yourself.'

The tall, conventional-looking barman finished pouring my beer and took my money. There was something in his tone of voice that made me determined to follow up this bizarre story.

Almost six months later, I found myself being ushered into a very small, dark room attached to the village church of Kampehl, where I went down a flight of steps and immediately stood over a large wooden coffin. The knight is not very tall and his hands appear to be clasped in a praying position. He is naked apart from a loincloth and still has teeth, some hair on his scalp and a penis. Veins are still visible beneath the dark brown hue of his leathery skin. I was unprepared for such a sight and clutched the sides of the coffin for support. Noticing my distress, the guardian of the mummified corpse, an old lady who was sitting in a dimly lit corner of the room, began to speak about the knight in a very slow but clear voice. His name was Christian Friedrich von Kahlbutz and he was born at Schloss zu Kampehl in 1651. A valiant knight, he was also a tyrant, an arrogant man who was obsessed with women and their sexual favours. He sired eleven children by one wife and was known to have fathered forty-four more from local girls. Amongst his many cruelties, he frequently insisted on his *droit de seigneur*, the feudal custom that allowed a lord to sleep with a peasant girl on the night of her wedding, to the anguish of her lawful bridegroom.

At one time there was a particularly beautiful girl that he lusted after, a young virgin by the name of Maria Leppin. She was betrothed to a young shepherd from the neighbouring village of Bückwitz, whom she loved dearly. Horrified by the knight's advances she dared to resist him and, because of his injured pride, the knight took his revenge on her fiancé, beating him to death one night in a field just outside the village. There were no eye witnesses but all the local people knew that it was Kahlbutz. Heartbroken, Maria accused him in front of the village and took him to court, but the evil lecher used his aristocratic powers to escape justice and moreover swore that if he was the murderer, 'then shall the good Lord never let my body rot'. He died in 1702, but it was not until 1794, when the church was being restored by the new lords of the manor, that their workmen opened the Kahlbutz family's mausoleum. Amongst the many coffins, they found the one containing the knight's incorrupt body. He had been condemned by his own curse and ever since it has been said that his soul can never rest.

By now I had all but recovered my composure and asked the old lady if it would be possible for me to photograph the corpse. She said that she did not have the authority to grant me permission and she did not think that anyone had ever been allowed to. My only hope was, she said, to ask the parish priest, who would be arriving at the church shortly for a service.

The clergyman was younger than I had expected and listened intensely, a Bible clutched to his breast, as I explained why I wanted to photograph this unholy libertine. The negotiations continued for a long time and it was not until I showed him some of my previous books that he finally allowed me to proceed. I began to position my tripod and very slowly the cadaver's skeletal features came into focus within the lens. I now felt distinctly vulnerable. Then the old lady began to tell me more of the legends that surround this unique phenomenon.

It is said that in 1806 some invading French soldiers found the knight's body, took it out of the coffin and tried to nail it to a large wooden cross in the church. However, as the soldiers were lifting him, one of the knight's arms swung backwards into the face of one of the soldiers and the unfortunate man died instantly of a heart attack. It is also recorded that in the 1900s the young men of the village would frighten the young girls by parading his body through the streets after dark and in one particular instance it was put into the bed of a honeymoon couple on their wedding night. Later, the corpse was rescued and stood upright in the waiting room of a doctor's surgery in nearby Neustadt for many years.

I asked the old lady how much of these stories was folklore and religious moralization. She smiled and said no one could be sure. All she knew was that in the early part of this century two eminent and well-respected pathologists, Virchow and Sauerbruch, had carried out an extensive autopsy on the body but failed to find any trace of embalming preservatives, and could not scientifically explain why the body had not decomposed. She added that many other medical experts have been unable to solve the mystery over the years.

Later, I went looking for the castle where the knight had been born, but could find no trace of it. All I could see was the ghostly, staring face of the 300-year-old cadaver that had earlier filled my lens.

THE NEEDLE OF DEATH

Lauenstein Castle, Bavaria

I came upon Lauenstein Castle by chance when travelling through the north of Bavaria towards the old East German border. I had spent the previous night in Bayreuth, where I had attended a performance of Wagner's dramatic opera *The Ring*, and my senses were very much alive to the world around me. It was early evening and the skies were clearing after a violent rainstorm when suddenly the castle appeared before me high above the dark forest, its pointed, fairytale towers reaching up towards the black clouds. Leaving the main road I drove up through a small village, entered the castle gates and continued up the driveway, but the great building seemed to be shuttered and deserted.

Katharina von Orlamünde took a very long, sharp needle and slowly pushed it into the brain of each of her children. She buried them herself, secretly, in the graveyard of a nunnery.

93

Parking the car, I approached the main door and rang the old-fashioned bell, but there was no reply. Disappointed, I began to walk back to my car, trying to work out how I could change my itinerary so that I could return, when the figure of a young girl with flowing blonde hair suddenly approached me as if from nowhere and introduced herself. She said that she helped with the occasional banquets that were held at the castle, which was now owned by the state, and that it was her turn to clear up after the festivities. She spoke very good English but it was her eyes that struck me most: they were as bright and alluring as any I had ever seen. She told me that the castle had originally been built by the Earls of Orlamünde in the twelfth century, but had changed hands many times since then. When I asked her whether there were any ghost stories attached to the old house she turned and stared at the castle and without hesitation began to recount the following story, which she said was recorded in ancient papers held at the castle since the sixteenth century and is widely known in the surrounding countryside.

A past lord of the castle, Graf Otto von Orlamünde, died in battle leaving a beautiful but headstrong young widow, Katharina von Orlamünde, and their two small children. After an appropriate period of mourning, she fell passionately in love with a certain Albrecht von Nürnberg, or 'Albert the Beautiful'. He had many other admirers and was not as infatuated with her as she was besotted by him. She used all her female powers to attract him, but then became convinced that her two small children would prevent her chances of marriage to him. She therefore decided to kill her two young children, but did not know how to commit the murders without anybody discovering her guilt. Finally, she took a very long, sharp needle and slowly pushed it into the brain of each child. There was barely a mark and she told her servants and friends that they had died of a mysterious illness. No one dared to question her and she secretly buried the bodies herself in the nearby nunnery at Himmelkron.

Within hours, she realized what she had done. She began to feel terrible remorse and, convinced that the local people would discover her crime, she decided to spend the rest of her life as a nun at the monastery. That way, she could be close to her loved ones; she would also escape possible arrest and execution. Her soul was to find no peace after death and her ghost still wanders through the ancient passages and vaults of the castle after twilight. She is dressed in white with a sad, pale expression and deep moans and sighs have been heard to precede this apparition. Her favourite haunt is the secret stairway to the main tower.

The girl seemed genuinely saddened by this story and when I asked if she had seen the ghost she did not seem to hear me. She simply walked back to the castle without even saying goodbye. Later, on reaching the bottom of the hill, I stopped to photograph the castle, now silhouetted by trees. In the peace and solitude of the forest it was hard not to feel a degree of pity for the tragic White Lady of Lauenstein, whose obsessive love condemned her endlessly to return to the scene of her crime.

Katharina was to find no peace after death and her ghost still wanders at twilight through the ancient passages and vaults of Lauenstein Castle. Her favourite haunt is the secret stairway to the great tower.

THE SHUTTERED ROOM

Falkenstein Castle, The Harz Mountains, Saxony-Anhalt

In 1969 I was given a book by my father called *The Confessions of a Ghost-Hunter* by Harry Price, the eminent and controversial psychical researcher. It covers many of his most interesting investigations of paranormal phenomena, including 'hauntings', one of which held a particular fascination for me. It concerned a castle in the Harz Mountains of Eastern Germany, which he had visited in the autumn of 1935, just as Hitler was arming Germany for war.

The Harz Mountains are associated with the supernatural in all its forms, and it is here, on the peak of the Brocken, that witches would meet on Walpurgis Night, 30 April, so vividly described by Goethe in the first part of *Faust*. The castle, Burg Falkenstein, dates back to the twelfth century and Price described it as 'one of the most beautiful specimens of a medieval residence I have ever seen'. Hidden from the outside world it lies in the middle of a forest perched on a rock 1,000 feet above sea level.

Inside the castle, Price was shown a small door with a massive iron lock. This door had not been opened for centuries and no one knew what the room beyond contained. Price was more interested, however, in another room, containing the Haunted Bed, a tall, wooden structure covered with ornately carved figures. This bedroom, and the bed itself, were said to be haunted by the White Lady of Falkenstein, reputed to be an ancestor of the present owner of the castle, Herr Graf von Asseburg. Price tried to gain permission from the old man to sleep overnight in the bed, but was refused, as the Earl did not want either the room, or the ghost, to be disturbed.

Shortly after Price's visit, the Second World War broke out and until recently the castle has been cut off from the western world. Now at last I hoped to see the Haunted Bed and discover the mystery of the Shuttered Room.

On my arrival in the mountains, I tried to follow the same route through the forest that Price had taken. The colour of the autumn leaves and the sight of so many different forms of wildlife was exhilarating. When it appeared, the castle was almost exactly as I had imagined it from Price's description and I was soon climbing the stone steps to an ancient wooden door, where I was greeted by one of the curators. Inside, it was as if nothing had changed for centuries, although it is now a state-run museum. It is full of antique furniture, strange artifacts and trophies of the chase.

As we followed the dark passages winding through the towers, I was told the castle's history. It was built by Burchard von Konradsburg in the twelfth century. He had originally lived in a castle at nearby Ermsleben but is said to have killed, some say

*H*arry Price (1881–1948), famous psychical researcher, whose visit to Falkenstein Castle inpired my interest in the Haunted Bed and the Shuttered Room.

*F*alkenstein Castle contains a mysterious room that remained locked for many years, concealing a terrible secret. In 1945, at the end of the Second World War, the door was smashed open by soldiers and the horror revealed.

murdered, Graf Adalbert Ballenstedt, and because of this tragedy converted his castle at Ermsleben into a monastery and changed his family's name to Valkenstein. Thus the building here was originally called Valkenstein castle and during the twelfth and thirteenth centuries the Valkenstein family became very powerful in the region. Later, for no known reason, they changed their name again, to Falkenstein. Perhaps they had something else to hide? In 1334 the family died out. The last member, who was a very religious man, but childless, gave the castle to the Abbey of Halberstadt. A century later the Abbey sold the castle to the Asseburg family, who owned it until 1945, the end of the Second World War.

We had now entered the room that contained the Haunted Bed that had so impressed Harry Price. It is much larger than I had imagined, a unique piece of sculpture that leaves one breathless with admiration. When I asked my guide about the ghost of the White Lady of Falkenstein she knew the legend, but was dismissive of the story and unwilling to add anything other than that the castle was mainly unoccupied at night so that there was no way of proving her existence. She did later add that another member of the staff would never enter the room because of something she had seen there.

Finally, we descended a winding set of stone steps to the private chapel where Martin Luther is said to have preached. Next to it is the Shuttered Room that Price was unable to enter almost sixty years ago. Now the door is open but much of the mystery of why it was kept locked for so long remains. It was originally a vestry, and was considered the most secure room in the castle as it only had a single door, and there were no windows. Entry would have been restricted to the priest and the owners of the castle,

In the castle it was as if nothing had changed for centuries, with rooms and passages full of antique furniture, artefacts and trophies of the chase.

and because it was so safe the deeds of the castle were kept here until 1604.

According to the present Earl of Asseburg, everybody in the area had always known that something or somebody was bricked up behind a wall in the room, but the exact truth was, and still is, a secret. He confirms that the deeds of the castle and other important documents were kept in the room until 1604, but then something happened to inspire the curse that the room should never be entered again by any living soul lest a great and terrible disaster should befall the Asseburg family.

A local legend persists that, in 1839, the door was opened and the room searched. Workmen were said to have discovered a cavity in one wall that contained a female skeleton wearing shreds of clothing. Her bones were later buried in nearby Pansfelde cemetery. This story has never been proved and there are many theories as to her identity. Either she was a human sacrifice to ward off evil spirits from the castle – a custom dating from Celtic times – or she had been a holy woman who had offered her life to redeem another's guilt, probably that of an aristocrat. This was a common practice in medieval times. The unfortunate victim would starve to death whilst praying for the soul of the guilty party. In return, their family would be financially rewarded. Other people claimed that she was a nun who had been bricked up alive for a sexual transgression or that she was the victim of a murder and had been concealed there. It is also said that when the skeleton was discovered, the Earl of Asseburg ordered that the room be sealed again.

Another story says that in 1910 a hole was made by mistake in the wall of the room near the church pulpit and the present Earl's grandmother, then a very inquisitive young woman, put her hand in one night and felt what she thought was a skeleton. It later turned out to be the leg of a carved chair. Then, in April 1945, towards the end of the Second World War, the American army arrived to occupy the castle, and the present Earl desperately tried to stop the troops opening the door. For the first few days he succeeded, then became ill with measles and was forced to take to his bed. One evening his young wife ran to his bedside shouting hysterically, 'The door has been smashed.' The following day a message came from nearby Ballenstedt, where his grandmother was living, saying that she had died at exactly the same time as the door had been broken down and the room entered – in the evening of 23 April 1945. Some weeks later the family were forced to flee the castle and the Fatherland.

Between the time of his grandmother's death and the family fleeing the country, the Earl, his wife, and his brother, thinking that they had nothing left to lose, plucked up courage and agreed to enter the room. They found the bunch of flowers that the wife had thrown in as the drunken soldiers smashed down the door; a carved wooden chair (the one that his grandmother had touched?); a hole in the floor, and beside it a large pile of earth; a workman's tressel and, finally, a cruel-looking butcher's hook hanging from a chain in the ceiling.

After nervously making my way through the dark corridors, I came to a richly tapestried bedroom. In the far corner stood a very large, ornate wooden bed, haunted by the White Lady of Falkenstein.

THE RESTLESS DEAD

Rothenberg Castle, Thuringia

As I was climbing the steep path up to this eerie castle my eyes caught a flash of light as the sharp blade of a woodman's axe rose and fell in the setting sun. I had heard mention of the ancient ruins from a local innkeeper the night before and approached the old man in the hope of learning something of their past. The sweat was pouring from his sunburnt forehead and as he wiped it away I noticed that he bore a long deep scar there. Pointing to the massive stone eagles perched on the castle walls, he said that it was known as Rothenberg Castle after its once powerful Lords, the Earls of Rothenberg, but they had fallen on hard times and it had been a ruin for many years. I asked him if it was haunted and he told me the following legend, which he said was centuries old.

When the Earls of Rothenberg were at the height of their powers they employed an old woman from the nearby village of Kelbra to bring them their food. She would carry it up to the castle each morning, sometimes returning to the village in the afternoon, sometimes in the early evening, and occasionally at midnight. If there was a full moon when she was going home, she would always meet the ghost of Sophie, Countess of Rothenberg, wandering through the woods below the castle, for she could find no rest. The old woman always asked her how she could help her and why she was so distraught, but the apparition would only beg her to make the following promise: if she should meet a tall man wearing a long black cloak and leading a fierce hound, to be sure to ask him how much longer she must still wander abroad as a restless spirit. When the old woman would later meet and ask this mysterious man, he always replied, 'Just one hundred years more.'

The woodman did not know the source of this legend but said that there was a later, nineteenth-century story that reinforced the castle's ghostly reputation. A local recluse took up residence in the only tower of the castle that was not a ruin. He was said to have been mad and the villagers kept away in fear. One day, during a bitterly cold winter, a passing farm boy found his body hanging from the tower window. He must have been dead for several days, but the castle's evil reputation, and his supposed insanity, had delayed the discovery. Beneath the tower were two sets of footprints in the deep snow; those of a tall man and a great hound. Since then, added the woodman, there have been several instances when inquisitive visitors to the old castle have seen 'something' that has made them flee in terror.

Did he believe these stories, I asked? He hesitated for a minute as if deep in thought, then slowly looked around him and back at me before giving his considered reply: 'I have never seen a ghost and pray that I never will.'

When the old woman returned to her village from the castle after delivering food, she would occasionally meet the ghost of Sophie, the Countess of Rothenberg. Sophie would request that the old woman find out how much longer she must wander abroad as a restless spirit.

ROMANIA

We are in Transylvania; and Transylvania is not England.
Our ways are not your ways,
and there shall be to you many strange things.
'Jonathan Harker's Journal', *Dracula*, Bram Stoker (1847–1912)

Before I travelled to Romania I was warned by a psychic against making the trip. When I asked him why, he said that it was not so much what might happen to me while I was there, but the evil I might bring back with me. I did not heed his advice but now think that I can understand exactly what he was referring to when he used the word 'evil', for the demonic figure of the real fifteenth-century Dracula, or Vlad Tepes (Vlad the Impaler), still casts a dark shadow across this beautiful, untamed country. Dracula's father, Vlad Dracul, was a descendant of the powerful Basarab dynasty and the word Dracul means 'Devil' or 'Dragon'.

From my arrival in Bucharest to my visit to Dracula's grave in the island monastery at Snagov, nothing in this wild land proved certain; everything had a double meaning and signs of the supernatural were everywhere. Driving through Romania can be depressing. The cities are disfigured by pollution and vast, empty concrete blocks of flats in which the country's most recent dictator, Nicolae Ceauşescu, was determined to imprison the peasants. However, these horrors are offset by the beauty of the wild mountains and also by the resplendent gypsies. Then one is reminded of the traveller's perilous predicament when passing one of the many roadside shrines, intended as sanctuaries from evil spirits, and as night falls the howling of wolves begins.

'I read that every known superstition in the world is gathered into the horseshoe of the Carpathians, as if it were the centre of some sort of imaginative whirlpool.' ('Jonathan Harker's Journal')

The Romanians are a Latin race who trace their ancestry through the Dacians and the Romans. Their belief in vampires, werewolves and the *strigoi* – a creature that is neither alive nor dead – runs through their folklore. It is easy to imagine these evil spirits roaming the wild countryside and the medieval villages and cities, many of which appear today as relics from a fairytale by the brothers Grimm. Romania has always had a large German population, and it was because of sensational rumours repeated by German traders who travelled through the country in the fifteenth century that the western world first heard of the notorious crimes of Dracula and his suspected vampirism.

Bram Stoker's Count Dracula was a masterpiece of invention, especially as he had no personal knowledge of Romania. But the Romanians see the real Dracula as a folk hero who saved their country from the invading Turks and their irritation with Stoker's imposter is real. I found the sites I visited frightening and this part of my journey, although exhilarating, was often also a waking nightmare that I hope will be laid to rest with this book.

THE DARK CASTLE

Corvin Castle, Hunedoara, Transylvania

Gradually, in front of me, through plumes of acrid grey and purple smoke, there appeared a multitude of fantastic towers and machiolations adorned with grotesque, leering gargoyles. This is Romania's greatest fortress, built in the fourteenth century by the Transylvanian warlord Iancu de Hunedoara, 'The White Knight', or János Hunyadi as he was known in Hungary. The black and sepulchral castle is surrounded by the worst excesses of decaying industry and it was easy to imagine that one had unsuspectingly wandered into the depths of a painting by Hieronymus Bosch. Surrounding the massive building is a precipitous moat over one hundred feet deep. Now, however, only a narrow stream of murky water remains, where the pale and ghostly figures of young children were swimming.

To enter the stronghold I had to cross the moat by a narrow wooden bridge, held up by precariously tall stone pillars. Happy to have survived this ordeal I passed through the towering gates to find myself within a vast and intimidating courtyard, off which led a maze of galleries, spiral stairways, Gothic vaults, deep dungeons and dark halls, the latter filled with great pillars and fading medieval tapestries. Everywhere pollution had added its ghastly stench and a layer of dust to the castle's aura of death.

It was in the most impressive of these chambers, the Knight's Hall, that I first heard mention of Dracula on my Romanian travels. The castle's female guide, a middle-aged woman with a distinctive limp, described how, as a devious young man, this future hero and demon of Romanian folklore had met and made an uneasy peace with Hunyadi, who in 1447 had been instrumental in the overthrow and murder of his father, Vlad Dracul. Dracula himself was later to be imprisoned for a short period by Hunyadi's warrior son Mátyás Corvin.

The legacy of horror and tales of torture that permeate the thick walls of the castle are legion. The guide pointed to one of the great marble pillars in the same hall and described how, in the fifteenth century, a young woman of the household was stripped naked, tied to the pillar, and a nail driven through her head after she was discovered to be having an illicit love affair with a lowly servant. Her bloodied apparition, dressed in white, is said to haunt the main tower and has been seen by the custodians of the castle as recently as 1990. During restoration works in 1873 a female skeleton was found beneath the tower stairs, its skull split in two by a rusted spike.

We then moved out into the courtyard again, where the guide led me to a deep and seemingly bottomless well. This, she said, had been dug by three unfortunate Turkish prisoners captured by Hunyadi's army. They were promised their freedom on

Mátyás Corvin a fearless warrior who imprisoned the infamous Dracula from 1462 to 1474. Opposite: Corvin Castle, Romania's greatest fortress, within whose now polluted ancient walls lurk dark secrets of murder and torture.

Previous pages: Dracula's Palace, Tîrgoviște, Wallachia, Romania.

In the castle's most impressive chamber, the Knight's Hall, I first heard mention of Dracula in Romania. I was told how the future hero and demon had made an uneasy peace here with Hunyadi, the murderer of his father, Vlad Dracul.

condition that they found water. Having dug with their bare hands for nine years to a depth of sixty feet they were finally successful, but by this time Hunyadi had died. His successors broke the bargain and the unfortunate men were thrown from the castle walls to drown in the moat below. Their names are still visible, carved into the rock near the base of the well, along with an inscription that reads, 'You have water but no soul.'

I was then shown an area of the castle which had been used as an amphitheatre, where prisoners were forced to fight bears and lions. If they lost, they were fed to them. She also told me that the prison beneath the main tower once contained a deep oubliette filled with over forty human skeletons and in an adjoining room there was a massive 'swinging blade' similar to that described in Edgar Allan Poe's 'The Pit and the Pendulum'. This horrific instrument of torture was said to have cut many prisoners to shreds.

When I asked her how the castle had finally become a ruin she replied that in 1854, after the last Corvin had sold all the furniture and treasures to pay off family debts, a terrible storm occurred one night and the building was struck by lightning. A fire broke out whilst the inhabitants were asleep and, apart from the walls, the only thing to survive was the thick wooden door to the tower prison. Everything and everybody else was consumed in the flames. The castle remained an abandoned ruin for some twenty years until restoration began.

I left feeling emotionally drained after so many horrific sights and stories, and my throat was sore from the mixture of chemical pollutants that I had inhaled. I was unashamedly relieved to hear the creaking of the rotting wood beneath my hesitant step as I crossed back over the ancient bridge.

By 1854 the last of the Corvins were at the end of their fortune. One night, during a terrible storm, the castle was struck by lightning and the inhabitants consumed by flames.

THE HIDDEN CORPSE

Bontida Castle, Transylvania

Cluj was once a provincial Hungarian city and much of its Baroque architecture remains as a reminder of the powerful Magyar families who once dominated this region of Transylvania. In the impressive History Museum I discovered a bizarre collection of artifacts, coats-of-arms and statuary commemorating the aristocratic and noble houses of the region. While gazing at a particularly striking, macabre figure of a man devouring a child, I was joined by a Romanian professor, who told me that the statue had been recovered from a castle outside Cluj that had belonged to the influential Bánffy dynasty. Telling him of my interest in ruins and the supernatural, he said that I could not fail to be inspired by this mansion. At one time, he added, there had been over forty similar statues at the house, known as Bontida Castle, but many had been destroyed or stolen.

I later discovered that the Bánffy family also built a palace in Cluj and a frequent visitor was their fellow countryman, the composer Franz Liszt (1811–66), who gave several concerts there. No doubt he would also have visited their country retreat at Bontida. Liszt's music was greatly influenced by Transylvania, and by the gypsies in particular; he even wrote a little-known, but compelling, study of their musical traditions, *The Gypsy in Music*.

Statue of the god Cronos devouring his own child, by J. Nachtigall. Recovered from Bontida Castle, the statue now stands in the History Museum of Transylvania in Cluj-Napoca.

As we left the northern outskirts of Cluj, carefully negotiating a path between the many horse-drawn carts and the deep potholes in the dusty road, I was trying to visualize the castle when I suddenly caught sight of my first gypsies. Many of these nomadic tribes have been assimilated into the mainstream Romanian population, but groups of these untouchables remain, carrying with them a secret knowledge that passes us by. I marvelled at their distinctive clothes, long dark hair and wild horses. These are troubadours whose pipes of Pan are reminders of their Indian, thirteenth-century origins. As worshippers of the sun and fire, they are credited with supernatural powers. My guide thought it interesting that a special relationship was said to have been forged between Dracula and a personal bodyguard of gypsies, whom he pardoned for their many crimes. He added that many gypsies enjoyed a similar status during Ceauşecu's reign, when they were absolved of serious offences, even murder. It would seem that this uneasy respect for the supernatural has always been rife in Romania, even amongst its tyrants, and in Bram Stoker's *Dracula* a pact existed between the Szgany tribe and the Count.

We continued our journey for another twenty miles before turning off the main road towards the castle, whose eerie silhouette now appeared on the horizon. Driving through the main gates I was immediately struck by the size of the estate and, as we

Embedded in the tall arch of what had once been a vast stable block at Bontida Castle, I found the remains of the Bánffy coat-of-arms.

Local people viewed the house, known as Bontida Castle, in awe, and approached it only timidly, if at all.

drew closer to the house, I noticed several broken statues scattered across the courtyard. On what had once been a vast stable block I found the remains of the Bánffy coat-of-arms embedded above the tall arch; in the distance stood the tall tower of a derelict chapel. Beyond lay a vast parkland, its many ancient trees populated by rooks who kept up a cacophony of sound as they watched our intrusion. No doubt this dark setting would have inspired Liszt, whose work shows a fascination with the macabre.

Clouds of dust swirled through the courtyard and within minutes of our arrival an almost constant stream of peasants began to walk towards us from the village, timidly approaching the house and staring up at it in awe, as if it had been built by the Gods. My guide asked them what they knew of its history and was told that the castle and grounds are now owned by the state (all large buildings and their lands in Romania were nationalized in 1947). Because they were Hungarian, the Bánffy family were unpopular landlords with many of the local people according to one old man, who added that they were so mean that nobody, not even a bird, was allowed within the castle's walls. Another man told how the last in line of the dynasty had been a novelist, who disagreed with the Nazis, who were occupying the country at the time and had seized the castle as their headquarters in the region. He published his views and, as a punishment, the Germans set fire to the house. He continued to say that a band of gypsies then inhabited the ruin for a short time, but left suddenly one night; nobody ever knew why. I decided to leave them talking to my guide while I took some photographs as the sky was darkening. As I wandered through the ruined buildings I felt frightened. What on earth, I wondered, was I expecting to find here?

In the great house I was confronted by a labyrinth of rooms that seemed to have no end, their crumbling white plaster adding a ghostly pallor to the ancient walls. As I pressed the shutter of the camera my guide suddenly appeared, insisting that I hear what an old lady had just told him. Apparently, the castle and grounds have had a ghostly reputation for many years. She remembered her father telling her that something tragic had happened here when he was a boy. The Bánffys were skilled horsemen and one of their daughters, a very beautiful and headstrong young girl, fell in love with a disreputable nobleman whose estate was nearby. She would often ride out to meet him in secret, but one of the family's grooms knew about her affair and, because he was jealous, threatened to tell her father. Desperate to keep the romance secret, she seduced the young boy and, during their lovemaking, stabbed him to death. She then buried his body somewhere on the estate. Something, said the old lady, probably the ghost of this unfortunate young man, has been seen in the buildings and grounds over the years. Nobody, it seems, has ever found his corpse, that his spirit might rest in peace. What had become of the girl, she did not know.

I suddenly wanted to leave and my guide agreed, saying that he found the atmosphere suffocating. Walking back to our car across the courtyard I noticed that the sky was now almost black and that the wind had suddenly dropped, the dust settling back over the ruins. Even the rooks had ceased their incessant cries; all had fallen silent in an uneasy calm. It was as if some terrible dark secret were about to be revealed.

In the distance stood the tall tower of the ruined family chapel (top). I began to feel frightened. What was I expecting to find here?
In the great house itself (right) were labyrinthine rooms, half destroyed. Where, I wondered, could the body of the unfortunate young boy have been hidden?

DRACULA'S CASTLE

Poienari Citadel, Argeş Valley, Wallachia

As we left the ancient town of Curtea de Argeş for Dracula's Castle, my guide seemed more apprehensive than usual, smoking heavily and glancing nervously around us as if we were being followed. The narrow road skirts the Argeş river, snaking through pastoral valleys that lie between wild crags and precipitous gorges. This is Dracula's country as I had imagined it and I began to feel as vulnerable as the unfortunate Jonathan Harker in Bram Stoker's novel. For many years now the Romanian tourist authorities have put forward the spectacular fortress of Bran in Transylvania as Dracula's lair, but it has only very tenuous associations with the folk hero. According to my guide, his actual castle at Poienari is thought to have been built in the fourteenth century during the reign of his ancestors the Basarab dynasty, but by the time Vlad came to the Wallachian throne it lay in ruins.

An episode in 1457 fully illustrated Dracula's ruthless nature. For some time he had suspected the loyalty of the boyars, or noblemen, in his capital city of Tîrgovişte, and when he discovered that they had buried alive one of his brothers he seized this opportunity to exact a terrible revenge on them. Two hundred of these aristocrats and their families were captured by Dracula's men after a church service on Easter Day. First the old men and their wives were impaled on the city walls, then the younger, more able-bodied were chained together and forced to march for sixty miles through the rugged countryside to the ruins of Poienari. Many of them died *en route*; the remainder were shattered, their fine clothes in tatters, some even naked. Lime kilns and brick ovens had been built in advance and the prisoners were forced to form a human chain under the whip to convey the building materials up the mountainside. The restoration work lasted for two months and very few of the captives survived the ordeal.

Dracula's statue stands in the park at Tîrgovişte. A cruel and ruthless man, most of the captive labour he used to restore his castle died during the ordeal.

Just as he was finishing this tale the dramatic and eerie remains of the castle came into view, perched precariously on top of a crag some 1,200 feet above the road. Even though only two of the original five towers remain (one third of the castle collapsed down the mountainside in 1888), it is an intimidating sight. My guide said that we could climb up the 1,440 steps to the summit, but as he was talking the earth shook with an almighty crash that sent us running for cover. We soon discovered that this was a controlled explosion to clear the road ahead, blocked by a landslide. We were both relieved to remain where we stood, and I began to photograph the castle from below.

Later, we spoke to several people in the nearby village of Arefu, where geese and pigs surrounded the ramshackle wooden houses. One old man told us how Dracula escaped from the castle when surrounded by the Turks. The night before the fortress was to be stormed, a loyal Romanian fired an arrow into the tower that contained Dracula's living quarters. It was found by his wife, who read the note and told him that she would 'rather have her body rot and be eaten by the fish of the Argeş than be led into captivity by the Turks'. She then flung herself from the battlements into the river below. But Dracula followed his scouts through a secret passage leading down to the river and, with the help of the local peasants, was able to flee to Transylvania. He is said to have rewarded the peasants who helped him by granting them lands here and confirmed this gift by writing the deeds on animal skins. The old man said that these skins were still in the possession of the men's families.

As we left the village we found ourselves at the rear of a funeral procession. The hearse was pulled by four black horses with purple plumes; the coffin was confined behind etched glass. Death, however, seemed all around us.

This is Dracula country as I imagined it from Bram Stoker's novel. The intimidating remains of Dracula's Castle loomed out of nowhere, perched on a crag some 1, 200 feet above the road.

DRACULA'S PALACE OF EVIL

The Princely Court of Tîrgovişte, Wallachia

In 1462 the invading army of the Sultan of Turkey, Mehmed 'the Conqueror', was preparing to attack Dracula's capital city of Tîrgovişte in the foothills of the Carpathian Mountains. According to the authors Florescu and McNally in their respected biography of Dracula, *Dracula, Prince of Many Faces*, the Greek chronicler Chalcondyles states:

'When they were some sixty miles north of the citadel their scouts reported a gruesome and horrific sight, which was later to become known during Dracula's reign of terror as "The Forest of the Impaled". Strung out along a mile or so in a huge semi-circle were thousands of stakes at various heights holding the remaining carcasses of some twenty thousand Turkish captives; their bodies were in a state of complete decomposition, due to the heat of the summer and the ravages of ravens and other Carpathian birds of prey, many of which had made their nests within the skulls and skeletal remains of their victims. The tattered remnants of their gaudy vestments fluttered against the evening sky. The entire area reeked with the stench of death – the smell of rotting flesh. The following morning the Sultan gave orders for his army to retreat.'

The 'wild beserker, Prince Dracula' dines at a table surrounded by his impaled and mutilated victims. From a sixteenth-century German pamphlet.

As you near the gates of Dracula's now-ruined palace at Tîrgovişte (he ruled from here as Voivode or Prince of Wallachia during three different periods in the fifteenth century), you are confronted by a large and intimidating bust of Vlad the Impaler, or Vlad Tepes as he was known to his countrymen. I stopped to photograph it, but was startled by a presence behind me. I turned and saw an old man, a beggar, who was wildly lunging his walking stick towards the sky. 'Tepes, Tepes,' he shouted and there was no doubt by his actions that he was imitating Dracula's favourite torture. As we were unable to understand each other further I gave him some money in return for his photograph; he then followed me to the palace gates but seemed unwilling to enter.

Very little remains of the actual state buildings except for the crumbling walls above the dark vaults, which contain kitchens, wine cellars, prisons and torture chambers; but dominating the princely court is the massive Chindia Watch Tower, which Dracula ordered to be built. Its principal function was to serve as a lookout for impending attack, but it also proved to be an ideal platform for the tyrant to watch the many impalements and tortures in the courtyard below. Our palace guide described some of Dracula's other horrific deeds. As well as his preference for impalement, he is said to

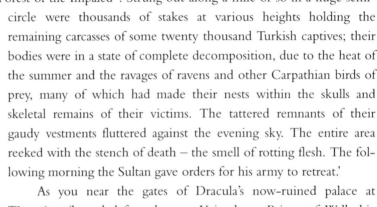

A large, intimidating bust of Dracula, or Vlad the Impaler, stands close to the gates of his now ruined palace, an ominous reminder of its dark history.

*D*racula invited the sick,
the blind and the poor to
a great dining hall in the
grounds of his princely
court, where a spectacular
feast was prepared for
them. Once they had eaten
and drunk their fill, he
burned them all to death.
Only crumbling walls
remain now of the palace
that witnessed this
terrible deed. The
princely chapel, however,
is well preserved.

have blinded, strangled, hanged, burned, skinned, roasted, hacked and buried alive men, women and children. She then gave me several ancient etchings depicting such deeds, including one where he is portrayed seated at a table, dining off a holy icon and surrounded by impaled and mutilated victims. It was as a result of this particularly shocking act, which took place near the city of Brasov in Transylvania, that Dracula's reputation as a cannibal and blood-drinking vampire began to gain credence. The guide added that, during his lifetime, he was said to have been responsible for the deaths of over 100,000 people, including one-third of the population of Wallachia.

One of his most obscene crimes took place in the Citadel of Tîrgoviște itself. He invited all the sick, the blind, the poor and the beggars of the region to a great dining hall, where a spectacular feast was prepared for them. After the many peasants had eaten their fill and drunk all the wine they could, Dracula ordered his men to set fire to the mansion. Not one of his guests survived the flames. Dracula then announced by decree that Wallachia was a great province, since it no longer accommodated such inadequate and useless people.

Later I was shown a secret tunnel that used to lead from the palace to the princely chapel. This remains a well-preserved, atmospheric and richly decorated shrine, a peaceful place where the monster would often retreat having indulged himself in an orgy of killing. He would then beg for forgiveness from God for his crimes, which he felt he was justified in committing for the good of the nation.

When I felt that I had seen and heard enough, I walked away from the remains of the palace into a field nearby, where I came across two stone crosses close to an ancient wall. I was reminded of the vampire's known aversion to a cross or crucifix and resolved to carry a crucifix with me during the remainder of my travels in Romania.

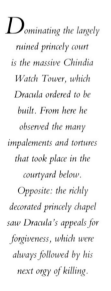

Dominating the largely ruined princely court is the massive Chindia Watch Tower, which Dracula ordered to be built. From here he observed the many impalements and tortures that took place in the courtyard below. Opposite: the richly decorated princely chapel saw Dracula's appeals for forgiveness, which were always followed by his next orgy of killing.

THE DEMON LAID TO REST?

Dracula's Grave, Snagov Monastery, Wallachia

I went through the door in the corner and down
the winding stair and along the dark passage to the old chapel.
I knew now well enough where to find the monster I sought.

'Jonathan Harker's Journal', *Dracula*, Bram Stoker (1847–1912)

Like so many of the legends surrounding Dracula's life, the circumstances of his death, and the subsequent accusations of vampirism, are shrouded in mystery. The end for Dracula came in the Vlasia forest, hidden in marshlands north of Bucharest. His headless and mutilated body was found by passing monks, who then took it to the island monastery of Snagov, where he was buried in front of the church altar. Some say that he was betrayed by his own countrymen seeking revenge, others that he was murdered by a hired Turkish assassin and his head presented to the Sultan in Constantinople, and some, of course, that he is not dead and that his spirit lives on as a vampire. The richly dressed body was exhumed in 1935 and this confirmed that it had been decapitated – interestingly, a widely recognized method of destroying a vampire. Both Dracula and his father had richly endowed the monastery during their lifetime and, furthermore, their dynasty had been closely associated with the building's violent and disturbing history for more than 150 years.

This, then, was the final prize, a visit to the tomb of the legendary 'Impaler'. It was in a mood of excited apprehension that my guide and I drove towards the lake through a maze of woods and unmarked roads. Finally we found ourselves in the marshlands and close to the shore of the beautiful lake. Surrounding us were a strange mixture of peasant shacks and the grandiose villas of ex-communist officials, the latter still guarded by edgy soldiers. We now began our search for someone who was willing to row us across to the island, but after hours of drawn-out negotiations with the local boatmen, it seemed that this was one instance where the offer of foreign money had no appeal. We decided that if this was the case, then we would stay the night nearby and try to find somebody who knew the people better and how exactly we should approach them. We found a somewhat ramshackle inn close to the shore and looked forward to our dinner and some local wine.

Our host was a large, gregarious man who clearly enjoyed the presence of a foreigner and was keen to tell me how the country had suffered under Ceauşescu, and how in the final years before the revolution the communist leader had begun to build a summer palace almost directly opposite the monastery where Dracula is said to rest. 'Perhaps they are blood brothers,' he added with a sly grin. When I began to question him further about the monastery, he told me how the local peasants believe the abbey and island to be haunted and that Dracula's curse still clings to the area. It is known that Snagov had a turbulent history and that Dracula rebuilt and fortified the monastery, and that his

This, then, was the route to the final prize, the tomb of the legendary Impaler. We drove through woods and unmarked roads to the island monastery.

Inside the monastery there was no sound. All was dark, save for the flickering of candles that at intervals lit up the rich gold and silver of the many icons. I could see the outline of a tomb in the stone floor, on which stood a vase of flowers, Dracula's portrait and an empty beaker.

half-brother Vlad 'The Monk' was abbot for a while. It is also believed that Dracula hid much of his treasure here, some of it at the bottom of the lake. In 1940, 1977, 1986 and 1990 the area suffered from earthquakes; during the nineteenth century it was turned into a prison. A bridge was built linking the island to the mainland and shortly after its construction it collapsed during a great storm, carrying a procession of chain-linked convicts to their death at the bottom of the lake. Their drowning screams and the rattle of the chains are said still to be heard. He then said that he would help us to find a boat in the morning and we wished him goodnight. Alone in my room, I lay in bed hoping to fall asleep quickly as I listened to the low whine of the first blood-sucking mosquito circling my head.

After breakfast we set out to meet a local fisherman whom our host thought our most likely ferryman, but once again we were to be disappointed; his boat had been stolen a few days before. By now the sky was beginning to darken and we could hear a distant growl of thunder. Suddenly, from behind some tall reeds, two peasant boys appeared and said that they would row us across. We quickly climbed into their boat and as we crossed the dark waters the island slowly appeared before us, surrounded by leaning willow trees. The monastery was scarred with great cracks, no doubt due to the earthquakes, and chickens and goats roamed freely between the outer buildings. We landed beside a rotting wooden jetty and told the two boys that we hoped to be no longer than an hour. They seemed unwilling to stay, but assured us they would return. We nervously approached the beautifully carved, half-open door of the monastery.

'His face was a strong – a very strong – aquiline, with high bridge of the thin nose and peculiarly arched nostrils . . . The mouth, so far as I could see it under the heavy moustache, was fixed and rather cruel-looking, with peculiarly sharp white teeth; these protruded over the lips, whose remarkable ruddiness showed astonishing vitality in a man of his years.' ('Jonathan Harker's Journal')

Inside, there was not a sound. All was dark, save for the flickering of candles that at intervals lit up the rich gold and silver of the many icons. Then, as I neared the altar, the small, dark figure of a nun appeared from behind a pillar and stared at me. 'Was this Dracula's grave?' I stammered. She did not reply, but continued to stare, I felt, straight through me. My Romanian guide intervened, asking the same question. 'Yes, it was Dracula's body,' she replied in a protective manner. 'We know this because when it was exhumed they found a ring and a buckle that had belonged to his father and that he had bequeathed, along with his sword, to his oldest surviving son, Dracula.' The guide then gave her some money and motioned towards me that I could take some photographs. The nun led me towards the altar where I saw the distinct outline of a tomb in the stone floor, on which stood a vase of flowers, Dracula's portrait and an empty beaker. The light was poor and I felt very nervous as the nun stood and watched me. I knew I was rushing the shot, but I somehow did not care; I just wanted to leave the monastery and island as quickly as possible.

After four or five minutes I nodded my thanks to the old lady, but she remained motionless. I walked to the door, turned once more and saw her making strange signs

over the grave, gesticulating and waving her arms as if in a trance. When we reached the boat, an old woman with very few teeth had taken the young boys' place. Climbing in, I tried to gather my thoughts, check that I had all my cameras. The sky was almost black and it was starting to rain. What, I wondered, had I done? 'The Vampire lives on,' wrote Bram Stoker, 'and cannot die by the mere passing of time.'

The piercing eyes of the King Vampire, the Prince of the Undead, still haunt this twilight land.

SELECT BIBLIOGRAPHY

Baigent, Michael, Richard Leigh & Henry Lincoln, *The Holy Blood and the Holy Grail*,
Jonathan Cape, London, 1982

Florescu, Radu R. & Raymond T. McNally, *Dracula, Prince of Many Faces*,
Little, Brown and Company, London, 1989

Fraser, Robert J. & William F. Rannie, *Arctic Adventurer*, Ontario, Canada, 1972

Iremonger, Lucille, *The Ghosts of Versailles*, Faber and Faber Ltd, London, 1957

Leigh Fermor, Patrick, *Between the Woods and the Water*, John Murray, London, 1986

Mackenzie, Andrew, *Dracula Country*, Arthur Barker, London, 1977

MacNeill, Máire, *Máire Rua, Lady of Leamaneh*, Ballinakella Press, Ireland, 1990

Price, Harry, *Confessions of a Ghost-Hunter*, Putnam, London, 1936

Ratazzi, Peter, *In Strangest Europe*, The Mitre Press, London, 1968

Sabau, Nicolae, *Sculptura Baroca in Romania,* Editura Meridiane, Bucharest, 1992

Sitwell, Sacheverell, *Romanian Journey*, Oxford University Press, Oxford, 1992

Tehou, Claude, *Guide De La Bourgogne et Du Lyonnais Mysterieux*,
Les Guides Noirs, Paris, 1974

Waldo-Schwartz, Paul, *Art and the Occult*, George Allen and Unwin Ltd, London, 1977

ACKNOWLEDGEMENTS

My thanks to the following for their assistance in compiling this book:
David Henderson, Tom Graves, Sadie Chowen, James Moores,
Professor Nicolae Sabau, Valerie Packenham, Duncan McLaren, David Berry,
Alison Rosse, Commander Michael Forsyth-Grant, Jan Lucas-Scudamore,
Joe Grenham, Michael Sweeney, Gerald Carroll, Donald Macer-Wright,
Marcel and Antoine Captier, Nicole Dawe and Celia Brooke.

A special thank-you to the following for their support, inspiration, humour and
invaluable practical help: Andrew Dennis, Malcolm Frazer, Christoph Graf von Spreti,
Marius Ghenea, Christian Gotsch, Vivien Bowler, Andrew Barron, Mari Roberts
and Lesley Baxter.

Thank you to Gray Levett of GRAYS OF WESTMINSTER – exclusively Nikon – for
supplying photographic equipment, and also to CLAN CAMPBELL WHISKEY for their
continued support.

Finally to my wife Cassie for her undying patience and support.

PICTURE CREDITS

Page 14 Ballinakella Press;
pp38, 48 Hulton Deutsch
Collection Ltd; p52 a & b
from *The Ghosts of
Versailles* by Lucille
Iremonger (by kind
permission of
Mrs Elspeth Milford and
Revd J. R. Jourdain); p66
by Émile Bayard, Explorer
Archives, France; p73 a &
b Museum of Rennes-le-
Château (Corbu-Captier
family); p78 Mary Evans
Picture Library; p86 from
portrait by S. J. Stump,
Hulton Deutsch
Collection Ltd; p96
University of London,
Harry Price
Collection/Marsden
Archive; p108 by
J. Nachtigall, History
Museum of Transylvania,
Cluj-Napoca/Marsden
Archive; p127 Tîrgovişte
Museum, Marsden
Archive.